Return to Rome

Jacques Casanova de Seingalt

[ZHINGOORA BOOKS]

This digital edition is published by Zhingoora Books.

The Cover is Designed by Pallav Sethiya.

zhingoora_books@yahoo.com

RETURN TO ROME

CHAPTER XIII

Rome—The Actor's Punishment—Lord Baltimore—Naples—Sara Goudar—Departure of Betty—Agatha—Medina—Albergoni—Miss Chudleigh—The Prince of Francavilla—The Swimmers

As I fell over the Englishman I had struck my hand against a nail, and the fourth finger of my left hand was bleeding as if a vein had been opened. Betty helped me to tie a handkerchief around the wound, while Sir B—— M—— read the letter with great attention. I was much pleased with Betty's action, it shewed she was confident, and sure of her lover's forgiveness.

I took up my coat and carpet-bag, and went into the next room to change my linen, and dress for dinner. Any distress at the termination of my intrigue with Betty was amply compensated for by my joy at the happy ending of a troublesome affair which might have proved fatal for me.

I dressed myself, and then waited for half an hour, as I heard Betty and Sir B—— M—— speaking in English calmly enough, and I did not care to interrupt them. At last the Englishman knocked at my door, and came in looking humble and mortified. He said he was sure I had not only saved Betty, but had effectually cured her of her folly.

"You must forgive my conduct, sir," said he, "for I could not guess that the man I found with her was her saviour and not her betrayer. I thank Heaven which inspired you with the idea of catching hold of me from behind, as I should certainly have killed you the moment I set eyes on you, and at this moment I should be the most wretched of men. You must forgive me, sir, and become my friend."

I embraced him cordially, telling him that if I had been in his place I should have acted in a precisely similar manner.

We returned to the room, and found Betty leaning against the bed, and weeping bitterly.

The blood continuing to flaw from my wound, I sent for a surgeon who said that a vein had been opened, and that a proper ligature was necessary.

Betty still wept, so I told Sir B—— M—— that in my opinion she deserved his forgiveness.

"Forgiveness?" said he, "you may be sure I have already forgiven her, and she well deserves it. Poor Betty repented directly you shewed her the path she was treading, and the tears she is shedding now are tears of sorrow at her mistake. I am sure she recognizes her folly, and will never be guilty of such a slip again."

Emotion is infectious. Betty wept, Sir B—— M—— wept, and I wept to keep them company. At last nature called a truce, and by degrees our sobs and tears ceased and we became calmer.

Sir B—— M——, who was evidently a man of the most generous character, began to laugh and jest, and his caresses had great effect in calming Betty. We made a good dinner, and the choice Muscat put us all in the best of spirits.

Sir B—— M—— said we had better rest for a day or two; he had journeyed fifteen stages in hot haste, and felt in need of repose.

He told us that on arriving at Leghorn, and finding no Betty there, he had discovered that her trunk had been booked to Rome, and that the officer to whom it belonged had hired a horse, leaving a watch as a pledge for it. Sir B—— M—— recognized Betty's watch, and feeling certain that she was either on horseback with her seducer or in the wagon with her trunk, he immediately resolved to pursue.

"I provided myself," he added, "with two good pistols, not with the idea of using one against her, for my first thought about her was pity, and my second forgiveness; but I determined to blow out the scoundrel's brains, and I mean to do it yet. We will start for Rome to-morrow."

Sir B—— M——'s concluding words filled Betty with joy, and I believe she would have pierced her perfidious lover to the heart if he had been brought before her at that moment.

"We shall find him at Roland's," said I.

Sir B—— M—— took Betty in his arms, and gazed at me with an air of content, as if he would have shewn me the greatness of an English heart—a greatness which more than atones for its weakness.

"I understand your purpose," I said, "but you shall not execute your plans without me. Let me have the charge of seeing that justice is done you. If you will not agree, I shall start for Rome directly, I shall get there before you, and shall give the wretched actor warning of your approach. If you had killed him before I should have said nothing, but at Rome it is different, and you would have reason to repent of having indulged your righteous indignation. You don't know Rome and priestly justice. Come, give me your hand and your word to do nothing without my consent, or else I shall leave you directly."

Sir B—— M—— was a man of my own height but somewhat thinner, and five or six years older; the reader will understand his character without my describing it.

My speech must have rather astonished him, but he knew that my disposition was benevolent, and he could not help giving me his hand and his pledge.

"Yes, dearest," said Betty, "leave vengeance to the friend whom Heaven has sent us."

"I consent to do so, provided everything is done in concert between us."

After this we parted, and Sir B—— M——, being in need of rest, I went to tell the vetturino that we should start for Rome again on the following day.

"For Rome! Then you have found your pocketbook? It seems to me, my good sir, that you would have been wiser not to search for it."

The worthy man, seeing my hand done up in lint, imagined I had fought a duel, and indeed everybody else came to the same conclusion.

Sir B—— M—— had gone to bed, and I spent the rest of the day in the company of Betty, who was overflowing with the gratitude. She said we must forget what had passed between us, and be the best of friends for the rest of our days, without a thought of any further amorous relations. I had not much difficulty in assenting to this condition.

She burned with the desire for vengeance on the scoundrelly actor who had deceived her; but I pointed out that her duty was to moderate Sir B—— M——'s passions, as if he attempted any violence in Rome it might prove a very serious matter for him, besides its being to the disadvantage of his reputation to have the affair talked of.

"I promise you," I added, "to have the rogue imprisoned as soon as we reach Rome, and that ought to be sufficient vengeance for you. Instead of the advantages he proposed for himself, he will receive only shame and all the misery of a prison."

Sir B—— M—— slept seven or eight hours, and rose to find that a good deal of his rage had evaporated. He consented to abide by my arrangements, if he could have the pleasure of paying the fellow a visit, as he wanted to know him.

After this sensible decision and a good supper I went to my lonely couch without any regret, for I was happy in the consciousness of having done a good action.

We started at day-break the next morning, and when we reached Acquapendente we resolved to post to Rome. By the post the journey took twelve hours, otherwise we should have been three days on the road.

As soon as we reached Rome I went to the customhouse and put in the document relating to Betty's trunk. The next day it was duly brought to our inn and handed over to Betty.

As Sir B—— M—— had placed the case in my hands I went to the bargello, an important person at Rome, and an expeditious officer when he sees a case clearly and feels sure that the plaintiffs do not mind spending their money. The bargello is rich, and lives well; he has an almost free access to the cardinal-vicar, the governor, and even the Holy Father himself.

He gave me a private interview directly, and I told him the whole story, finally saying that all we asked for was that the rogue should be imprisoned and afterwards expelled from Rome.

"You see," I added, "that our demand is a very moderate one, and we could get all we want by the ordinary channels of the law; but we are in a hurry, and I want you to take charge of the whole affair. If you care to do so we shall be prepared to defray legal expenses to the extent of fifty crowns."

The bargello asked me to give him the bill of exchange and all the effects of the adventurer, including the letters.

I had the bill in my pocket and gave it him on the spot, taking a receipt in exchange. I told him to send to the inn for the rest.

"As soon as I have made him confess the facts you allege against him," said the bargello, "we shall be able to do something. I have already heard that he is at Roland's, and has been trying to get the Englishwoman's trunk. If you liked to spend a hundred crowns instead of fifty we could send him to the galleys for a couple of years."

"We will see about that," said I, "for the present we will have him into prison."

He was delighted to hear that the horse was not l'Etoile's property, and said that if I liked to call at nine o'clock he would have further news for me.

I said I would come. I really had a good deal to do at Rome. I wanted to see Cardinal Bernis in the first place, but I postponed everything to the affair of the moment.

I went back to the inn and was told by a valet de place, whom Sir B—— M—— had hired, that the Englishman had gone to bed.

We were in need of a carriage, so I summoned the landlord and was astonished to find myself confronted by Roland in person.

"How's this?" I said. "I thought you were still at the Place d'Espagne."

"I have given my old house to my daughter who has married a prosperous Frenchman, while I have taken this palace where there are some magnificent rooms."

"Has your daughter many foreigners staying at her house now?"

"Only one Frenchman, the Comte de l'Etoile, who is waiting for his equipage to come on. He has an excellent horse, and I am thinking of buying it from him."

"I advise you to wait till to-morrow, and to say nothing about the advice
I have given you."

"Why should I wait?"

"I can't say any more just now."

This Roland was the father of the Therese whom I had loved nine years before, and whom my brother Jean had married in 1762, a year after my departure. Roland told me that my brother was in Rome with Prince Beloselski, the Russian ambassador to the Court of Saxony.

"I understood that my brother could not come to Rome."

"He came with a safe-conduct which the Dowager Electress of Saxony obtained for him from the Holy Father. He wants his case to be re-tried, and there he makes a mistake, for if it were heard a hundred times the sentence would continue the same. No one will see him, everyone avoids him, even Mengs will have nothing to say to him."

"Mengs is here, is he? I though he had been at Madrid."

"He has got leave of absence for a year, but his family remains in Spain."

After hearing all this news which was far from pleasant to me, as I did not wish to see Mengs or my brother, I went to bed, leaving orders that I was to be roused in time for dinner.

In an hour's time I was awakened by the tidings that some one was waiting to give me a note. It was one of the bargello's men, who had come to take over L'Etoile's effects.

At dinner I told Sir B—— M—— what I had done, and we agreed that he should accompany me to the bargello's in the evening.

In the afternoon we visited some of the principal palaces, and after taking Betty back to the inn we went to the bargello, who told us our man was already in prison, and that it would cost very little to send him to the galleys.

"Before making up my mind I should like to speak to him," said Sir
B—— M——.

"You can do so to-morrow. He confessed everything without any trouble, and made a jest of it, saying he was not afraid of any consequences, as the young lady had gone with him of her own free will. I shewed him the bill of exchange, but he evinced no emotion whatever. He told me that he was an actor by profession, but also a man of rank. As to the horse, he said he was at perfect liberty to sell it, as the watch he had left in pledge was worth more than the beast."

I had forgotten to inform the bargello that the watch aforesaid belonged to Betty.

We gave the worthy official fifty crowns, and supped with Betty, who had, as I have remarked, recovered her trunk, and had been busying herself in putting her things to rights.

She was glad to hear that the rascal was in prison, but she did not seem to wish to pay him a visit.

We went to see him in the afternoon of the next day.

The bargello had assigned us an advocate, who made out a document demanding payment by the prisoner of the expenses of the journey, and of his arrest, together with a certain sum as compensation to the person whom he had deceived, unless he could prove his right to the title of count in the course of six weeks.

We found L'Etoile with this document in his hand; someone was translating it for him into French.

As soon as the rascal saw me, he said, with a laugh, that I owed him twenty-five Louis as he had left Betty to sleep with me.

The Englishman told him he lied; it was he that had slept with her.

"Are you Betty's lover?" asked L'Etoile.

"Yes, and if I had caught you with her I should have blown out your brains, for you have deceived her doubly; you're only a beggarly actor."

"I have three thousand crowns."

"I will pay six thousand if the bill proves to be a good one. In the meanwhile you will stay here, and if it be false, as I expect it is, you will go to the galleys."

"Very good."

"I shall speak to my counsel."

We went out and called on the advocate, for Sir B—— M—— had a lively desire to send the impudent rascal to the galleys. However, it could not be done, for l'Etoile said he was quite ready to give up the bill, but that he expected Sir B—— M—— to pay a crown a day for his keep while he remained in prison.

Sir B—— M—— thought he would like to see something of Rome, as he was there, and was obliged to buy almost everything as he had left his belongings behind him, while Betty was well provided for as her trunk was of immense capacity. I went with them everywhere; it was not exactly the life I liked, but there would be time for me to please myself after they had gone. I loved Betty without desiring her, and I had taken a liking to the Englishman who had an excellent heart. At first he wanted to stay a fortnight at Rome, and then to return to Leghorn; but his friend Lord Baltimore, who had come to Rome in the meanwhile, persuaded him to pay a short visit to Naples.

This nobleman, who had with him a very pretty Frenchwoman and two servants, said he would see to the journey, and that I must join the party. I had made his acquaintance at London.

I was glad to have the opportunity of seeing Naples again. We lodged at the "Crocielles" at Chiaggia, or Chiaja, as the Neapolitans call it.

The first news I heard was the death of the Duke of Matalone and the marriage of his widow with Prince Caramanica.

This circumstance put an end to some of my hopes, and I only thought of amusing myself with my friends, as if I had never been at Naples before. Lord Baltimore had been there several times, but his mistress, Betty, and Sir B—— M——, were strangers, and wanted to see everything. I accordingly acted as cicerone, for which part I and my lord, too, were much better qualified than the tedious and ignorant fellows who had an official right to that title.

The day after our arrival I was unpleasantly surprised to see the notorious Chevalier Goudar, whom I had known at London. He called on Lord Baltimore.

This famous rout had a house at Pausilippo, and his wife was none other than the pretty Irish girl Sara, formerly a drawer in a London tavern. The reader has been already introduced to her. Goudar knew I had met her, so he told me who she was, inviting us all to dine with him the next day.

Sara skewed no surprise nor confusion at the sight of me, but I was petrified. She was dressed with the utmost elegance, received company admirably, spoke Italian with perfect correctness, talked sensibly, and was exquisitely beautiful; I was stupefied; the metamorphosis was so great.

In a quarter of an hour five or six ladies of the highest rank arrived, with ten or twelve dukes, princes, and marquises, to say nothing of a host of distinguished strangers.

The table was laid for thirty, but before dinner Madame Goudar seated herself at the piano, and sang a few airs with the voice of a siren, and with a confidence that did not astonish the other guests as they knew her, but which astonished me extremely, for her singing was really admirable.

Goudar had worked this miracle. He had been educating her to be his wife for six or seven years.

After marrying her he had taken her to Paris, Vienna, Venice, Florence, Rome, etc., everywhere seeking fortune, but in vain. Finally he had come to Naples, where he had brought his wife into the fashion of obliging her to renounce in public the errors of the Anglican heresy. She had been received into the Catholic Church under the auspices of the Queen of Naples. The amusing part in all this was that Sara, being an Irishwoman, had been born a Catholic, and had never ceased to be one.

All the nobility, even to the Court, went to see Sara, while she went nowhere, for no one invited her. This kind of thing is a characteristic of nobility all the world over.

Goudar told me all these particulars, and confessed that he only made his living by gaming. Faro and biribi were the only pillars of his house; but they must have been strong ones, for he lived in great style.

He asked me to join with him, and I did not care to refuse; my purse was fast approaching total depletion, and if it were not for this resource I could not continue living in the style to which I had been accustomed.

Having taken this resolution I declined returning to Rome with Betty and Sir B—— M——, who wanted to repay me all I had spent on her account. I was not in a position to be ostentatious, so I accepted his generous offer.

Two months later I heard that l'Etoile had been liberated by the influence of Cardinal Bernis, and had left Rome. Next year I heard at Florence that Sir B—— M—— had returned to England, where no doubt he married Betty as soon as he became a widower.

As for the famous Lord Baltimore he left Naples a few days after my friends, and travelled about Italy in his usual way. Three years later he paid for his British bravado with his life. He committed the wild imprudence of traversing the Maremma in August, and was killed by the poisonous exhalations.

I stopped at "Crocielles," as all the rich foreigners came to live there. I was thus enabled to make their acquaintance, and put them in the way of losing their money at Goudar's. I did not like my task, but circumstances were too strong for me.

Five or six days after Betty had left I chanced to meet the Abby Gama, who had aged a good deal, but was still as gay and active as ever. After we had told each other our adventures he informed me that, as all the differences between the Holy See and the Court of Naples had been adjusted, he was going back to Rome.

Before he went, however, he said he should like to present me to a lady whom he was sure I should be very glad to see again.

The first persons I thought of were Donna Leonilda, or Donna Lucrezia, her mother; but what was my surprise to see Agatha, the dancer with whom I had been in love at Turin after abandoning the Corticelli.

Our delight was mutual, and we proceeded to tell each other the incidents of our lives since we had parted.

My tale only lasted a quarter of an hour, but Agatha's history was a long one.

She had only danced a year at Naples. An advocate had fallen in love with her, and she shewed me four pretty children she had given him. The husband came in at supper-time, and as she had often talked to him about me he rushed to embrace me as soon as he heard my name. He was an intelligent man, like most of the pagletti of Naples. We supped together like old friends, and the Abbe Gama going soon after supper I stayed with them till midnight, promising to join them at dinner the next day.

Although Agatha was in the very flower of her beauty, the old fires were not rekindled in me. I was ten years older. My coolness pleased me, for I should not have liked to trouble the peace of a happy home.

After leaving Agatha I proceeded to Goudar's, in whose bank I took a strong interest. I found a dozen gamesters round the table, but what was my surprise to recognize in the holder of the bank Count Medini.

Three or four days before this Medini had been expelled from the house of M. de Choiseul, the French ambassador; he had been caught cheating at cards. I had also my reason to be incensed against him; and, as the reader may remember, we had fought a duel.

On glancing at the bank I saw that it was at the last gasp. It ought to have held six hundred ounces, and there were scarcely a hundred. I was interested to the extent of a third.

On examining the face of the punter who had made these ravages I guessed the game. It was the first time I had seen the rascal at Goudar's.

At the end of the deal Goudar told me that this punter was a rich Frenchman who had been introduced by Medini. He told me I should not mind his winning that evening, as he would be sure to lose it all and a good deal more another time.

"I don't care who the punter is," said I, "it is not of the slightest consequence to me, as I tell you plainly that as long as Medini is the banker I will have nothing to do with it."

"I have told Medini about it and wanted to take a third away from the bank, but he seemed offended and said he would make up any loss to you, but that he could not have the bank touched."

"Very good, but if he does not bring me my money by to-morrow morning there will be trouble. Indeed, the responsibility lies with you, for I have told you that as long as Medini deals I will have nothing to do with it."

"Of course you have a claim on me for two hundred ounces, but I hope you will be reasonable; it would be rather hard for me to lose two-thirds."

Knowing Goudar to be a greater rascal than Medini, I did not believe a word he said; and I waited impatiently for the end of the game.

At one o'clock it was all over. The lucky punter went off with his pockets full of gold, and Medini, affecting high spirits, which were very much out of place, swore his victory should cost him dear.

"Will you kindly give me my two hundred ounces," said I, "for, of course,
Gondar told you that I was out of it?"

"I confess myself indebted to you for that amount, as you absolutely insist, but pray tell me why you refuse to be interested in the bank when I am dealing."

"Because I have no confidence in your luck."

"You must see that your words are capable of a very unpleasant interpretation."

"I can't prevent your interpreting my words as you please, but I have a right to my own opinion. I want my two hundred ounces, and I am quite willing to leave you any moneys you propose to make out of the conqueror of to-night. You must make your arrangements with M. Goudar, and by noon to-morrow, you, M. Goudar, will bring me that sum."

"I can't remit you the money till the count gives it me, for I haven't got any money."

"I am sure you will have some money by twelve o'clock to-morrow morning.
Goodnight."

I would not listen to any of their swindling arguments, and went home without the slightest doubt that they were trying to cheat me. I resolved to wash my hands of the whole gang as soon as I had got my money back by fair means or foul.

At nine the next morning I received a note from Medini, begging me to call on him and settle the matter. I replied that he must make his arrangements with Goudar, and I begged to be excused calling on him.

In the course of an hour he paid me a visit, and exerted all his eloquence to persuade me to take a bill for two hundred ounces, payable in a week. I gave him a sharp refusal, saying that my business was with Goudar and Gondar only, and that unless I received the money by noon I should proceed to extremities. Medini raised his voice, and told me that my language was offensive; and forthwith I took up a pistol and placed it against his cheek, ordering him to leave the room. He turned pale, and went away without a word.

At noon I went to Gondar's without my sword, but with two good pistols in my pocket. Medini was there, and began by reproaching me with attempting to assassinate him in my own house.

I took no notice of this, but told Gondar to give me my two hundred ounces.

Goudar asked Medini to give him the money.

There would undoubtedly have been a quarrel, if I had not been prudent enough to leave the room, threatening Gondar with ruin if he did not send on the money directly.

Just as I was leaving the house, the fair Sara put her head out of the window, and begged me to come up by the back stairs and speak to her.

I begged to be excused, so she said she would come down, and in a moment she stood beside me.

"You are in the right about your money," she said, "but just at present my husband has not got any; you really must wait two or three days, I will guarantee the payment."

"I am really sorry," I replied, "not to be able to oblige such a charming woman, but the only thing that will pacify me is my money, and till I have had it, you will see me no more in your house, against which I declare war."

Thereupon she drew from her finger a diamond ring, worth at least four hundred ounces, and begged me to accept it as a pledge.

I took it, and left her after making my bow. She was doubtless astonished at my behaviour, for in her state of deshabille she could not have counted on my displaying such firmness.

I was very well satisfied with my victory, and went to dine with the advocate, Agatha's husband. I told him the story, begging him to find someone who would give me two hundred ounces on the ring.

"I will do it myself," said he; and he gave me an acknowledgment and two hundred ounces on the spot. He then wrote in my name a letter to Goudar, informing him that he was the depositary of the ring.

This done, I recovered my good temper.

Before dinner Agatha took me into her boudoir and shewed me all the splendid jewels I had given her when I was rich and in love.

"Now I am a rich woman," said she, "and my good fortune is all your making; so take back what you gave me. Don't be offended; I am so grateful to you, and my good husband and I agreed on this plan this morning."

To take away any scruples I might have, she shewed me the diamonds her husband had given her; they had belonged to his first wife and were worth a considerable sum.

My gratitude was too great for words, I could only press her hand, and let my eyes speak the feelings of my heart. Just then her husband came in.

It had evidently been concerted between them, for the worthy man embraced me, and begged me to accede to his wife's request.

We then joined the company which consisted of a dozen or so of their friends, but the only person who attracted my attention was a very young man, whom I set down at once as in love with Agatha. His name was Don Pascal Latilla; and I could well believe that he would be successful in love, for he was intelligent, handsome, and well-mannered. We became friends in the course of the meal.

Amongst the ladies I was greatly pleased with one young girl. She was only fourteen, but she looked eighteen. Agatha told me she was studying singing, intending to go on the stage as she was so poor.

"So pretty, and yet poor?"

"Yes, for she will have all or nothing; and lovers of that kind are rare in Naples."

"But she must have some lover?"

"If she has, no one has heard of him. You had better make her acquaintance and go and see her. You will soon be friends."

"What's her name?"

"Callimena. The lady who is speaking to her is her aunt, and I expect they are talking about you."

We sat down to the enjoyment of a delicate and abundant meal. Agatha, I could see, was happy, and delighted to shew me how happy she was. The old Abbe Gama congratulated himself on having presented me. Don Pascal Latilla could not be jealous of the attentions paid me by his idol, for I was a stranger, and they were my due; while her husband prided himself on his freedom from those vulgar prejudices to which so many Neapolitans are subject.

In the midst of all this gaiety I could not help stealing many a furtive glance towards Callimena. I addressed her again and again, and she answered me politely but so briefly as to give me no opportunity of displaying my powers in the way of persiflage.

I asked if her name was her family name or a pseudonym.

"It is my baptismal name."

"It is Greek; but, of course, you know what it means?"

"No."

"Mad beauty, or fair moon."

"I am glad to say that I have nothing in common with my name."

"Have you any brothers or sisters?"

"I have only one married sister, with whom you may possibly be acquainted."

"What is her name, and who is her husband?"

"Her husband is a Piedmontese, but she does not live with him."

"Is she the Madame Slopis who travels with Aston?"

"Exactly."

"I can give you good news of her."

After dinner I asked Agatha how she came to know Callimena.

"My husband is her godfather."

"What is her exact age?"

"Fourteen."

"She's a simple prodigy! What loveliness!"

"Her sister is still handsomer."

"I have never seen her."

A servant came in and said M. Goudar would like to have a little private conversation with the advocate.

The advocate came back in a quarter of an hour, and informed me that Goudar had given him the two hundred ounces, and that he had returned him the ring.

"Then that's all settled, and I am very glad of it. I have certainly made an eternal enemy of him, but that doesn't trouble me much."

We began playing, and Agatha made me play with Callimena, the freshness and simplicity of whose character delighted me.

I told her all I knew about her sister, and promised I would write to Turin to enquire whether she were still there. I told her that I loved her, and that if she would allow me, I would come and see her. Her reply was extremely satisfactory.

The next morning I went to wish her good day. She was taking a music lesson from her master. Her talents were really of a moderate order, but love made me pronounce her performance to be exquisite.

When the master had gone, I remained alone with her. The poor girl overwhelmed me with apologies for her dress, her wretched furniture, and for her inability to give me a proper breakfast.

"All that make you more desirable in my eyes, and I am only sorry that I cannot offer you a fortune."

As I praised her beauty, she allowed me to kiss her ardently, but she stopped my further progress by giving me a kiss as if to satisfy me.

I made an effort to restrain my ardour, and told her to tell me truly whether she had a lover.

"Not one."

"And have you never had one?"

"Never."

"Not even a fancy for anyone?"

"No, never."

"What, with your beauty and sensibility, is there no man in Naples who has succeeded in inspiring you with desire?"

"No one has ever tried to do so. No one has spoken to me as you have, and that is the plain truth."

"I believe you, and I see that I must make haste to leave Naples, if I would not be the most unhappy of men."

"What do you mean?"

"I should love you without the hope of possessing you, and thus I should be most unhappy."

"Love me then, and stay. Try and make me love you. Only you must moderate your ecstacies, for I cannot love a man who cannot exercise self-restraint."

"As just now, for instance?"

"Yes. If you calm yourself I shall think you do so for my sake, and thus love will tread close on the heels of gratitude."

This was as much as to tell me that though she did not love me yet I had only to wait patiently, and I resolved to follow her advice. I had reached an age which knows nothing of the impatient desires of youth.

I gave her a tender embrace, and as I was getting up to go I asked her if she were in need of money.

This question male her blush, and she said I had better ask her aunt, who was in the next room.

I went in, and was somewhat astonished to find the aunt seated between two worthy Capuchins, who were talking small talk to her while she worked at her needle. At a little distance three young girls sat sewing.

The aunt would have risen to welcome me, but I prevented her, asked her how she did, and smilingly congratulated her on her company. She smiled back, but the Capuchins sat as firm as two stocks, without honouring me with as much as a glance.

I took a chair and sat down beside her.

She was near her fiftieth year, though some might have doubted whether she would ever see it again; her manner was good and honest, and her features bore the traces of the beauty that time had ruined.

Although I am not a prejudiced man, the presence of the two evil-smelling monks annoyed me extremely. I thought the obstinate way in which they stayed little less than an insult. True they were men like myself, in spite of their goats' beards and dirty frocks, and consequently were liable to the same desires as I; but for all that I found them wholly intolerable. I could not shame them without shaming the lady, and they knew it; monks are adepts at such calculations.

I have travelled all over Europe, but France is the only country in which
I saw a decent and respectable clergy.

At the end of a quarter of an hour I could contain myself no longer, and told the aunt that I wished to say something to her in private. I thought the two satyrs would have taken the hint, but I counted without my host. The aunt arose, however, and took me into the next room.

I asked my question as delicately as possible, and she replied,—

"Alas! I have only too great a need of twenty ducats (about eighty francs) to pay my rent."

I gave her the money on the spot, and I saw that she was very grateful, but I left her before she could express her feelings.

Here I must tell my readers (if I ever have any) of an event which took place on that same day.

As I was dining in my room by myself, I was told that a Venetian gentleman who said he knew me wished to speak to me.

I ordered him to be shewn in, and though his face was not wholly unknown to me I could not recollect who he was.

He was tall, thin and wretched, misery and hunger spewing plainly in his every feature; his beard was long, his head shaven, his robe a dingy brown, and bound about him with a coarse cord, whence hung a rosary and a dirty handkerchief. In the left hand he bore a basket, and in the right a long stick; his form is still before me, but I think of him not as a humble penitent, but as a being in the last state of desperation; almost an assassin.

"Who are you?" I said at length. "I think I have seen you before, and yet . . ."

"I will soon tell you my name and the story of my woes; but first give me something to eat, for I am dying of hunger. I have had nothing but bad soup for the last few days."

"Certainly; go downstairs and have your dinner, and then come back to me; you can't eat and speak at the same time."

My man went down to give him his meal, and I gave instructions that I was not to be left alone with him as he terrified me.

I felt sure that I ought to know him, and longed to hear his story.

In three quarters of an hour he came up again, looking like some one in a high fever.

"Sit down," said I, "and speak freely."

"My name is Albergoni."

"What!"

Albergoni was a gentleman of Padua, and one of my most intimate friends twenty-five years before. He was provided with a small fortune, but an abundance of wit, and had a great leaning towards pleasure and the exercise of satire. He laughed at the police and the cheated husbands, indulged in Venus and Bacchus to excess, sacrificed to the god of pederasty, and gamed incessantly. He was now hideously ugly, but when I knew him first he was a very Antinous.

He told me the following story:

"A club of young rakes, of whom I was one, had a casino at the Zuecca; we passed many a pleasant hour there without hurting anyone. Some one imagined that these meetings were the scenes of unlawful pleasures, the engines of the law were secretly directed against us, and the casino was shut up, and we were ordered to be arrested. All escaped except myself and a man named Branzandi. We had to wait for our unjust sentence for two years, but at last it appeared. My wretched fellow was condemned to lose his head, and afterwards to be burnt, while I was sentenced to ten years' imprisonment 'in carcere duro'. In 1765 I was set free, and went to Padua hoping to live in peace, but my persecutors gave me no rest, and I was accused of the same crime. I would not wait for the storm to burst, so I fled to Rome, and two years afterwards the Council of Ten condemned me to perpetual banishment.

"I might bear this if I had the wherewithal to live, but a brother-in-law of mine has possessed himself of all I have, and the unjust Tribunal winks at his misdeeds.

"A Roman attorney made me an offer of an annuity of two pawls a day on the condition that I should renounce all claims on my estate. I refused this iniquitous condition, and left Rome to come here and turn hermit. I have followed this sorry trade for two years, and can bear it no more."

"Go back to Rome; you can live on two pawls a day."

"I would rather die."

I pitied him sincerely, and said that though I was not a rich man he was welcome to dine every day at my expense while I remained in Naples, and I gave him a sequin.

Two or three days later my man told me that the poor wretch had committed suicide.

In his room were found five numbers, which he bequeathed to Medini and myself out of gratitude for our kindness to him. These five numbers were very profitable to the Lottery of Naples, for everyone, myself excepted, rushed to get them. Not a single one proved a winning number, but the popular belief that numbers given by a man before he commits suicide are infallible is too deeply rooted among the Neapolitans to be destroyed by such a misadventure.

I went to see the wretched man's body, and then entered a cafe. Someone was talking of the case, and maintaining that death by strangulation must be most luxurious as the victim always expires with a strong erection. It might be so, but the erection might also be the result of an agony of pain, and before anyone can speak dogmatically on the point he must first have had a practical experience.

As I was leaving the cafe I had the good luck to catch a handkerchief thief in the act; it was about the twentieth I had stolen from me in the month I had spent at Naples. Such petty thieves abound there, and their skill is something amazing.

As soon as he felt himself caught, he begged me not to make any noise, swearing he would return all the handkerchiefs he had stolen from me, which, as he confessed, amounted to seven or eight.

"You have stolen more than twenty from me."

"Not I, but some of my mates. If you come with me, perhaps we shall be able to get them all back."

"Is it far off?"

"In the Largo del Castello. Let me go; people are looking at us."

The little rascal took me to an evil-looking tavern, and shewed me into a room, where a man asked me if I wanted to buy any old things. As soon as he heard I had come for my handkerchiefs, he opened a big cupboard full of handkerchiefs, amongst which I found a dozen of mine, and bought them back for a trifle.

A few days after I bought several others, though I knew they were stolen.

The worthy Neapolitan dealer seemed to think me trustworthy, and three or four days before I left Naples he told me that he could sell me, for ten or twelve thousand ducats, commodities which would fetch four times that amount at Rome or elsewhere.

"What kind of commodities are they?"

"Watches, snuff-boxes, rings, and jewels, which I dare not sell here."

"Aren't you afraid of being discovered?"

"Not much, I don't tell everyone of my business."

I thanked him, but I would not look at his trinkets, as I was afraid the temptation of making such a profit would be too great.

When I got back to my inn I found some guests had arrived, of whom a few were known to me. Bartoldi had arrived from Dresden with two young Saxons, whose tutor he was. These young noblemen were rich and handsome, and looked fond of pleasure.

Bartoldi was an old friend of mine. He had played Harlequin at the King of Poland's Italian Theatre. On the death of the monarch he had been placed at the head of the opera-buffa by the dowager electress, who was passionately fond of music.

Amongst the other strangers were Miss Chudleigh, now Duchess of Kingston, with a nobleman and a knight whose names I have forgotten.

The duchess recognized me at once, and seemed pleased that I paid my court to her. An hour afterwards Mr. Hamilton came to see her, and I was delighted to make his acquaintance. We all dined together. Mr. Hamilton was a genius, and yet he ended by marrying a mere girl, who was clever enough to make him in love with her. Such a misfortune often comes to clever men in their old age. Marriage is always a folly; but when a man marries a young woman at a time of life when his physical strength is running low, he is bound to pay dearly for his folly; and if his wife is amorous of him she will kill him even years ago I had a narrow escape myself from the same fate.

After dinner I presented the two Saxons to the duchess; they gave her news of the dowager electress, of whom she was very fond. We then went to the play together. As chance would have it, Madame Goudar occupied the box next to ours, and Hamilton amused the duchess by telling the story of the handsome Irishwoman, but her grace did not seem desirous of making Sara's acquaintance.

After supper the duchess arranged a game of quinze with the two Englishmen and the two Saxons. The stakes were small, and the Saxons proved victorious. I had not taken any part in the game, but I resolved to do so the next evening.

The following day we dined magnificently with the Prince of Francavilla, and in the afternoon he took us to the bath by the seashore, where we saw a wonderful sight. A priest stripped himself naked, leapt into the water, and without making the slightest movement floated on the surface like a piece of deal. There was no trick in it, and the marvel must be assigned to some special quality in his organs of breathing. After this the prince amused the duchess still more pleasantly. He made all his pages, lads of fifteen to seventeen, go into the water, and their various evolutions afforded us great pleasure. They were all the sweethearts of the prince, who preferred Ganymede to Hebe.

The Englishmen asked him if if he would give us the same spectacle, only substituting nymphs for the 'amoyini', and he promised to do so the next day at his splendid house near Portici, where there was a marble basin in the midst of the garden.

CHAPTER XIV

My Amours with Gallimena—Journey to Soyento—Medini—Goudar—Miss Chudleigh—The Marquis Petina—Gaetano—Madame Cornelis's Son—An Anecdote of Sara Goudar—The Florentines Mocked by the King—My Journey to Salerno, Return to Naples, and Arrival at Rome

The Prince of Francavilla was a rich Epicurean, whose motto was 'Fovet et favet'.

He was in favour in Spain, but the king allowed him to live at Naples, as he was afraid of his initiating the Prince of Asturias, his brothers, and perhaps the whole Court, into his peculiar vices.

The next day he kept his promise, and we had the pleasure of seeing the marble basin filled with ten or twelve beautiful girls who swam about in the water.

Miss Chudleigh and the two other ladies pronounced this spectacle tedious; they no doubt preferred that of the previous day.

In spite of this gay company I went to see Callimena twice a day; she still made me sigh in vain.

Agatha was my confidante; she would gladly have helped me to attain my ends, but her dignity would not allow of her giving me any overt assistance. She promised to ask Callimena to accompany us on an excursion to Sorento, hoping that I should succeed in my object during the night we should have to spend there.

Before Agatha had made these arrangements, Hamilton had made similar ones with the Duchess of Kingston, and I succeeded in getting an invitation. I associated chiefly with the two Saxons and a charming Abbe Guliani, with whom I afterwards made a more intimate acquaintance at Rome.

We left Naples at four o'clock in the morning, in a felucca with twelve oars, and at nine we reached Sorrento.

We were fifteen in number, and all were delighted with this earthly paradise.

Hamilton took us to a garden belonging to the Duke of Serra Capriola, who chanced to be there with his beautiful Piedmontese wife, who loved her husband passionately.

The duke had been sent there two months before for having appeared in public in an equipage which was adjudged too magnificent. The minister Tanucci called on the king to punish this infringement of the sumptuary laws, and as the king had not yet learnt to resist his ministers, the duke and his wife were exiled to this earthly paradise. But a paradise which is a prison is no paradise at all; they were both dying of ennui, and our arrival was balm in Gilead to them.

A certain Abbe Bettoni, whose acquaintance I had made nine years before at the late Duke of Matalone's, had come to see them, and was delighted to meet me again.

The abbe was a native of Brescia, but he had chosen Sorento as his residence. He had three thousand crowns a year, and lived well, enjoying all the gifts of Bacchus, Ceres, Comus, and Venus, the latter being his favourite divinity. He had only to desire to attain, and no man could desire greater pleasure than he enjoyed at Sorento. I was vexed to see Count Medini with him; we were enemies, and gave each other the coldest of greetings.

We were twenty-two at table and enjoyed delicious fare, for in that land everything is good; the very bread is sweeter than elsewhere. We spent the afternoon in inspecting the villages, which are surrounded by avenues finer than the avenues leading to the grandest castles in Europe.

Abbe Bettoni treated us to lemon, coffee, and chocolate ices, and some delicious cream cheese. Naples excels in these delicacies, and the abbe had everything of the best. We were waited on by five or six country girls of ravishing beauty, dressed with exquisite neatness. I asked him whether that were his seraglio, and he replied that it might be so, but that jealousy was unknown, as I should see for myself if I cared to spend a week with him.

I envied this happy man, and yet I pitied him, for he was at least twelve years older than I, and I was by no means young. His pleasures could not last much longer.

In the evening we returned to the duke's, and sat down to a supper composed of several kinds of fish.

The air of Sorento gives an untiring appetite, and the supper soon disappeared.

After supper my lady proposed a game at faro, and Bettoni, knowing Medini to be a professional gamester, asked him to hold the bank. He begged to be excused, saying he had not enough money, so I consented to take his place.

The cards were brought in, and I emptied my poor purse on the table. It only held four hundred ounces, but that was all I possessed.

The game began; and on Medini asking me if I would allow him a share in the bank, I begged him to excuse me on the score of inconvenience.

I went on dealing till midnight, and by that time I had only forty ounces left. Everybody had won except Sir Rosebury, who had punted in English bank notes, which I had put into my pocket without counting.

When I got to my room I thought I had better look at the bank notes, for the depletion of my purse disquieted me. My delight may be imagined. I found I had got four hundred and fifty pounds—more than double what I had lost.

I went to sleep well pleased with my day's work, and resolved not to tell anyone of my good luck.

The duchess had arranged for us to start at nine, and Madame de Serra
Capriola begged us to take coffee with her before going.

After breakfast Medini and Bettoni came in, and the former asked Hamilton whether he would mind his returning with us. Of course, Hamilton could not refuse, so he came on board, and at two o'clock I was back at my inn. I was astonished to be greeted in my antechamber by a young lady, who asked me sadly whether I remembered her. She was the eldest of the five Hanoverians, the same that had fled with the Marquis dells Petina.

I told her to come in, and ordered dinner to be brought up.

"If you are alone," she said, "I should be glad to share your repast."

"Certainly; I will order dinner for two."

Her story was soon told. She had come to Naples with her husband, whom her mother refused to recognize. The poor wretch had sold all he possessed, and two or three months after he had been arrested on several charges of forgery. His poor mate had supported him in prison for seven years. She had heard that I was at Naples, and wanted me to help her, not as the Marquis della Petina wished, by lending him money, but by employing my influence with the Duchess of Kingston to make that lady take her to England with her in her service.

"Are you married to the marquis?"

"No."

"Then how could you keep him for seven years?"

"Alas . . . . You can think of a hundred ways, and they would all be true."

"I see."

"Can you procure me an interview with the duchess?"

"I will try, but I warn you that I shall tell her the simple truth."

"Very good."

"Come again to-morrow."

At six o'clock I went to ask Hamilton how I could exchange the English notes I had won, and he gave me the money himself.

Before supper I spoke to the duchess about the poor Hanoverian. My lady said she remembered seeing her, and that she would like to have a talk with her before coming to any decision. I brought the poor creature to her the next day, and left them alone. The result of the interview was that the duchess took her into her service in the place of a Roman girl, and the Hanoverian went to England with her. I never heard of her again, but a few days after Petina sent to beg me to come and see him in prison, and I could not refuse. I found him with a young man whom I recognized as his brother, though he was very handsome and the marquis very ugly; but the distinction between beauty and ugliness is often hard to point out.

This visit proved a very tedious one, for I had to listen to a long story which did not interest me in the least.

As I was going out I was met by an official, who said another prisoner wanted to speak to me.

"What's his name?"

"His name is Gaetano, and he says he is a relation of yours."

My relation and Gaetano! I thought it might be the abbe.

I went up to the first floor, and found a score of wretched prisoners sitting on the ground roaring an obscene song in chorus.

Such gaiety is the last resource of men condemned to imprisonment on the galleys; it is nature giving her children some relief.

One of the prisoners came up to me and greeted me as "gossip." He would have embraced me, but I stepped back. He told me his name, and I recognized in him that Gaetano who had married a pretty woman under my auspices as her godfather. The reader may remember that I afterwards helped her to escape from him.

"I am sorry to see you here, but what can I do for you?"

"You can pay me the hundred crowns you owe me, for the goods supplied to you at Paris by me."

This was a lie, so I turned my back on him, saying I supposed imprisonment had driven him mad.

As I went away I asked an official why he had been imprisoned, and was told it was for forgery, and that he would have been hanged if it had not been for a legal flaw. He was sentenced to imprisonment for life.

I dismissed him from my mind, but in the afternoon I had a visit from an advocate who demanded a hundred crowns on Gaetano's behalf, supporting his claim by the production of an immense ledger, where my name appeared as debtor on several pages.

"Sir," said I, "the man is mad; I don't owe him anything, and the evidence of this book is utterly worthless.

"You make a mistake, sir," he replied; "this ledger is good evidence, and our laws deal very favorably with imprisoned creditors. I am retained for them, and if you do not settle the matter by to-morrow I shall serve you with a summons."

I restrained my indignation and asked him politely for his name and address. He wrote it down directly, feeling quite certain that his affair was as good as settled.

I called on Agatha, and her husband was much amused when I told my story.

He made me sign a power of attorney, empowering him to act for me, and he then advised the other advocate that all communications in the case must be made to him alone.

The 'paglietti' who abound in Naples only live by cheating, and especially by imposing on strangers.

Sir Rosebury remained at Naples, and I found myself acquainted with all the English visitors. They all lodged at "Crocielles," for the English are like a flock of sheep; they follow each other about, always go to the came place, and never care to shew any originality. We often arranged little trips in which the two Saxons joined, and I found the time pass very pleasantly. Nevertheless, I should have left Naples after the fair if my love for

Callimena had not restrained me. I saw her every day and made her presents, but she only granted me the slightest of favours.

The fair was nearly over, and Agatha was making her preparations for going to Sorento as had been arranged. She begged her husband to invite a lady whom he had loved before marrying her while she invited Pascal Latilla for herself, and Callimena for me.

There were thus three couples, and the three gentlemen were to defray all expenses.

Agatha's husband took the direction of everything.

A few days before the party I saw, to my surprise, Joseph, son of Madame
Cornelis and brother of my dear Sophie.

"How did you come to Naples? Whom are you with?"

"I am by myself. I wanted to see Italy, and my mother gave me this pleasure. I have seen Turin, Milan, Genoa, Florence, Venice, and Rome; and after I have done Italy I shall see Switzerland and Germany, and then return to England by way of Holland."

"How long is this expedition to take?"

"Six months."

"I suppose you will be able to give a full account of everything when you go back to London?"

"I hope to convince my mother that the money she spent was not wasted."

"How much do you think it will cost you?"

"The five hundred guineas she gave me, no more."

"Do you mean to say you are only going to spend five hundred guineas in six months? I can't believe it."

"Economy works wonders."

"I suppose so. How have you done as to letters of introduction in all these countries of which you now know so much?"

"I have had no introductions. I carry an English passport, and let people think that I am English."

"Aren't you afraid of getting into bad company?"

"I don't give myself the chance. I don't speak to anyone, and when people address me I reply in monosyllables. I always strike a bargain before I eat a meal or take a lodging. I only travel in public conveyances."

"Very good. Here you will be able to economize; I will pay all your expenses, and give you an excellent cicerone, one who will cost you nothing."

"I am much obliged, but I promised my mother not to accept anything from anybody."

"I think you might make an exception in my case."

"No. I have relations in Venice, and I would not take so much as a single dinner from them. When I promise, I perform."

Knowing his obstinacy, I did not insist. He was now a young man of twenty-three, of a delicate order of prettiness, and might easily have been taken for a girl in disguise if he had not allowed his whiskers to grow.

Although his grand tour seemed an extravagant project, I could not help admiring his courage and desire to be well informed.

I asked him about his mother and daughter, and he replied to my questions without reserve.

He told me that Madame Cornelis was head over ears in debts, and spent about half the year in prison. She would then get out by giving fresh bills and making various arrangements with her creditors, who knew that if they did not allow her to give her balls, they could not expect to get their money.

My daughter, I heard, was a pretty girl of seventeen, very talented, and patronized by the first ladies in London. She gave concerts, but had to bear a good deal from her mother.

I asked him to whom she was to have been married, when she was taken from the boarding school. He said he had never heard of anything of the kind.

"Are you in any business?"

"No. My mother is always talking of buying a cargo and sending me with it to the Indies, but the day never seems to come, and I am afraid it never will come. To buy a cargo one must have some money, and my mother has none."

In spite of his promise, I induced him to accept the services of my man, who shewed him all the curiosities of Naples in the course of a week.

I could not make him stay another week. He set out for Rome, and wrote to me from there that he had left six shirts and a great coat behind him. He begged me to send them on, but he forgot to give me his address.

He was a hare-brained fellow, and yet with the help of two or three sound maxims he managed to traverse half Europe without coming to any grief.

I had an unexpected visit from Goudar, who knew the kind of company I kept, and wanted me to ask his wife and himself to dinner to meet the two Saxons and my English friends.

I promised to oblige him on the understanding that there was to be no play at my house, as I did not want to be involved in any unpleasantness. He was perfectly satisfied with this arrangement, as he felt sure his wife would attract them to his house, where, as he said, one could play without being afraid of anything.

As I was going to Sorento the next day, I made an appointment with him for a day after my return.

This trip to Sorento was my last happy day.

The advocate took us to a house where we were lodged with all possible comfort. We had four rooms; the first was occupied by Agatha and her husband, the second by Callimena and the advocate's old sweetheart, the third by Pascal Latilla, and the fourth by myself.

After supper we went early to bed, and rising with the sun we went our several ways; the advocate with his old sweetheart, Agatha with Pascal, and I with Callimena. At noon we met again to enjoy a delicious dinner, and then the advocate took his siesta, while Pascal went for a walk with Agatha and her husband's sweetheart, and I wandered with Callimena under the shady alleys where the heat of the sun could not penetrate. Here it was that Callimena consented to gratify my passion. She gave herself for love's sake alone, and seemed sorry she had made me wait so long.

On the fourth day we returned to Naples in three carriages, as there was a strong wind. Callimena persuaded me to tell her aunt what had passed between us, that we might be able to meet without any restraint for the future.

I approved of her idea, and, not fearing to meet with much severity from the aunt, I took her apart and told her all that had passed, making her reasonable offers.

She was a sensible woman, and heard what I had to say with great good humour. She said that as I seemed inclined to do something for her niece, she would let me know as soon as possible what she wanted most. I remarked that as I should soon be leaving for Rome, I should like to sup with her niece every evening. She thought this a very natural wish on my part, and so we went to Callimena, who was delighted to hear the result of our interview.

I lost no time, but supped and passed that night with her. I made her all my own by the power of my love, and by buying her such things as she most needed, such as linen, dresses, etc. It cost me about a hundred louis, and in spite of the smallness of my means I thought I had made a good bargain. Agatha, whom I told of my good luck, was delighted to have helped me to procure it.

Two or three days after I gave a dinner to my English friends, the two
Saxons, Bartoldi their governor, and Goudar and his wife.

We were all ready, and only waiting for M. and Madame Goudar, when I saw the fair Irishwoman come in with Count Medini. This piece of insolence made all the blood in my body rush to my head. However, I restrained myself till Goudar came in, and then I gave him a piece of my mind. It had been agreed that his wife should come with him. The rascally fellow prevaricated, and tried hard to induce me to believe that Medini had not plotted the breaking of the bank, but his eloquence was in vain.

Our dinner was a most agreeable one, and Sara cut a brilliant figure, for she possessed every pleasing quality that can make a woman attractive. In good truth, this tavern girl would have filled a throne with any queen; but Fortune is blind.

When the dinner was over, M. de Buturlin, a distinguished Russian, and a great lover of pretty women, paid me a visit. He had been attracted by the sweet voice of the fair Sara, who was singing a Neapolitan air to the guitar. I shone only with a borrowed light, but I was far from being offended. Buturlin fell in love with Sara on the spot, and a few months after I left he got her for five hundred Louis, which Goudar required to carry out the order he had received, namely, to leave Naples in three days.

This stroke came from the queen, who found out that the king met Madame Goudar secretly at Procida. She found her royal husband laughing heartily at a letter which he would not shew her.

The queen's curiosity was excited, and at last the king gave in, and her majesty read the following:

"Ti aspettero nel medesimo luogo, ed alla stessa ora, coll' impazienza medesima che ha una vacca che desidera l'avicinamento del toro."

"Chi infamia!" cried the queen, and her majesty gave the cow's husband to understand that in three days he would have to leave Naples, and look for bulls in other countries.

If these events had not taken place, M. de Buturlin would not have made so good a bargain.

After my dinner, Goudar asked all the company to sup with him the next evening. The repast was a magnificent one, but when Medini sat down at the end of a long table behind a heap of gold and a pack of cards, no punters came forward. Madame Goudar tried in vain to make the gentlemen take a hand. The Englishmen and the Saxons said politely that they should be delighted to play if she or I would take the bank, but they feared the count's extraordinary fortune.

Thereupon Goudar had the impudence to ask me to deal for a fourth share.

"I will not deal under a half share," I replied, "though I have no confidence in my luck."

Goudar spoke to Medini, who got up, took away his share, and left me the place.

I had only two hundred ounces in my purse. I placed them beside Goudar's two hundred, and in two hours my bank was broken, and I went to console myself with my Callimena.

Finding myself penniless I decided to yield to the pressure of Agatha's husband, who continued to beg me to take back the jewelry I had given his wife. I told Agatha I would never have consented if fortune had been kinder to me. She told her husband, and the worthy man came out of his closet and embraced me as if I had just made his fortune.

I told him I should like to have the value of the jewels, and the next day I found myself once more in possession of fifteen thousand francs. From that moment I decided to go to Rome, intending to stop there for eight months; but before my departure the advocate said he must give me a dinner at a casino which he had at Portici.

I had plenty of food for thought when I found myself in the house where I had made a small fortune by my trick with the mercury five-and-twenty years ago.

The king was then at Portici with his Court, and our curiosity attracting us we were witnesses of a most singular spectacle.

The king was only nineteen and loved all kinds of frolics. He conceived a desire to be tossed in a blanket! Probably few crowned heads have wished to imitate Sancho Panza in this manner.

His majesty was tossed to his heart's content; but after his aerial journeys he wished to laugh at those whom he had amused. He began by proposing that the queen should take part in the game; on her replying by shrieks of laughter, his majesty did not insist.

The old courtiers made their escape, greatly to my regret, for I should have liked to see them cutting capers in the air, specially Prince Paul Nicander, who had been the king's tutor, and had filled him with all his own prejudices.

When the king saw that his old followers had fled, he was reduced to asking the young nobles present to play their part.

I was not afraid for myself, as I was unknown, and not of sufficient rank to merit such an honour.

After three or four young noblemen had been tossed, much to the amusement of the queen and her ladies, the king cast his eyes on two young Florentine nobles who had lately arrived at Naples. They were with their tutor, and all three had been laughing heartily at the disport of the king and his courtiers.

The monarch came up and accosted them very pleasantly, proposing that they should take part in the game.

The wretched Tuscans had been baked in a bad oven; they were undersized, ugly, and humpbacked.

His majesty's proposal seemed to put them on thorns. Everybody listened for the effects of the king's eloquence; he was urging them to undress, and saying that it would be unmannerly to refuse; there could be no humiliation in it, he said, as he himself had been the first to submit.

The tutor felt that it would not do to give the king a refusal, and told them that they must give in, and thereupon the two Florentines took off their clothes.

When the company saw their figures and doleful expressions, the laughter became general. The king took one of them by the hand, observing in an encouraging manner that there would be no danger; and as a special honour he held one of the corners of the blanket himself. But, for all that, big tears rolled down the wretched young man's cheeks.

After three or four visits to the ceiling, and amusing everyone by the display of his long thin legs, he was released, and the younger brother went to the torture smilingly, for which he was rewarded by applause.

The governor, suspecting that his majesty destined him for the same fate, had slipped out; and the king laughed merrily when he heard of his departure.

Such was the extraordinary spectacle we enjoyed—a spectacle in every way unique.

Don Pascal Latilla, who had been lucky enough to avoid his majesty's notice, told us a number of pleasant anecdotes about the king; all shewed him in the amiable light of a friend of mirth and an enemy to all pomp and stateliness, by which kings are hedged in generally. He assured us that no one could help liking him, because he always preferred to be treated as a friend rather than a monarch.

"He is never more grieved," said Pascal, "than when his minister Tanucci shews him that he must be severe, and his greatest joy is to grant a favour."

Ferdinand had not the least tincture of letters, but as he was a man of good sense he honoured lettered men most highly, indeed anyone of merit was sure of his patronage. He revered the minister Marco, he had the greatest respect for the memory of Lelio Caraffa, and of the Dukes of Matalone, and he had provided handsomely for a nephew of the famous man of letters Genovesi, in consideration of his uncle's merits.

Games of chance were forbidden; and one day he surprised a number of the officers of his guard playing at faro. The young men were terrified at the sight of the king, and would have hidden their cards and money.

"Don't put yourselves out," said the kindly monarch, "take care that
Tanucci doesn't catch you, but don't mind me."

His father was extremely fond of him up to the time when he was obliged to resist the paternal orders in deference to State reasons.

Ferdinand knew that though he was the King of Spain's son, he was none the less king of the two Sicilies, and his duties as king had the prerogative over his duties as son.

Some months after the suppression of the Jesuits, he wrote his father a letter, beginning:

"There are four things which astonish me very much. The first is that though the Jesuits were said to be so rich, not a penny was found upon them at the suppression; the second, that though the Scrivani of Naples are supposed to take no fees, yet their wealth is immense; the third, that while all the other young couples have children sooner or later, we have none; and the fourth, that all men die at last, except Tanucci, who, I believe, will live on in 'saecula saeculorum'."

The King of Spain shewed this letter to all the ministers and ambassadors, that they might see that his son was a clever man, and he was right; for a man who can write such a letter must be clever.

Two or three days later, the Chevalier de Morosini, the nephew of the procurator, and sole heir of the illustrious house of Morosini, came to Naples accompanied by his tutor Stratico, the professor of mathematics at Padua, and the same that had given me a letter for his brother, the Pisan professor. He stayed at the "Crocielles," and we were delighted to see one another again.

Morosini, a young man of nineteen, was travelling to complete his education. He had spent three years at Turin academy, and was now under the superintendence of a man who could have introduced him to the whole range of learning, but unhappily the will was wanting in the pupil. The young Venetian loved women to excess, frequented the society of young rakes, and yawned in good company. He was a sworn foe to study, and spent his money in a lavish manner, less from generosity than from a desire to be revenged on his uncle's economies. He complained of being still kept in tutelage; he had calculated that he could spend eight hundred sequins a month, and thought his allowance of two hundred sequins a month an insult. With this notion, he set himself to sow debts broadcast, and only laughed at his tutor when he mildly reproached him for his extravagance, and pointed out that if he were saving for the present, he would be able to be all the more magnificent on his return to Venice. His uncle had made an excellent match for him; he was to marry a girl who was extremely pretty, and also the heiress of the house of Grimani de Servi.

The only redeeming feature in the young man's character was that he had a mortal hatred of all kinds of play.

Since my bank had been broken I had been at Goudar's, but I would not listen to his proposal that I should join them again. Medini had become a sworn foe of mine. As soon as I came, he would go away, but I pretended not to notice him. He was at Goudar's when I introduced Morosini and his mentor, and thinking the young man good game he became very intimate with him. When he found out that Morosini would not hear of gaming, his hatred of me increased, for he was certain that I had warned the rich Venetian against him.

Morosini was much taken with Sara's charms, and only thought of how he could possess her. He was still a young man, full of romantic notions, and she would have become odious in his eyes if he could have guessed that she would have to be bought with a heavy price.

He told me several times that if a woman proposed payment for her favours, his disgust would expel his love in a moment. As he said, and rightly, he was as good a man as Madame Goudar was a woman.

This was distinctly a good point in his character; no woman who gave her favours in exchange for presents received could hope to dupe him. Sara's maxims were diametrically opposed to his; she looked on her love as a bill of exchange.

Stratico was delighted to see him engaged in this intrigue, for the chief point in dealing with him was to keep him occupied. If he had no distractions he took refuge in bad company or furious riding. He would sometimes ride ten or twelve stages at full gallop, utterly ruining the horses. He was only too glad to make his uncle pay for them, as he swore he was an old miser.

After I had made up my mind to leave Naples, I had a visit from Don Pascal Latilla, who brought with him the Abbe Galiani, whom I had known at Paris.

It may be remembered that I had known his brother at St. Agatha's,   where
I had stayed with him, and left him Donna Lucrezia Castelli.

I told him that I had intended to visit him, and asked if Lucrezia were still with him.

"She lives at Salerno," said he, "with her daughter the Marchioness C——."

I was delighted to hear the news; if it had not been for the abbe's visit, I should never have heard what had become of these ladies.

I asked him if he knew the Marchioness C——.

"I only know the marquis," he replied, "he is old and very rich."

That was enough for me.

A couple of days afterwards Morosini invited Sara, Goudar, two young gamesters, and Medini, to dinner. The latter had not yet given up hopes of cheating the chevalier in one way or another.

Towards the end of dinner it happened that Medini differed in opinion from me, and expressed his views in such a peremptory manner that I remarked that a gentleman would be rather more choice in his expressions.

"Maybe," he replied, "but I am not going to learn manners from you."

I constrained myself, and said nothing, but I was getting tired of his insolence; and as he might imagine that my resentment was caused by fear, I determined on disabusing him.

As he was taking his coffee on the balcony overlooking the sea, I came up to him with my cup in my hand, and said that I was tired of the rudeness with which he treated me in company.

"You would find me ruder still," he replied, "if we could meet without company."

"I think I could convince you of your mistake if we could have a private meeting."

"I should very much like to see you do it."

"When you see me go out, follow me, and don't say a word to anyone."

"I will not fail."

I rejoined the company, and walked slowly towards Pausilippo. I looked back and saw him following me; and as he was a brave fellow, and we both had our swords, I felt sure the thing would soon be settled.

As soon as I found myself in the open country, where we should not be interrupted, I stopped short.

As he drew near I attempted a parley, thinking that we might come to a more amicable settlement; but the fellow rushed on me with his sword in one hand and his hat in the other.

I lunged out at him, and instead of attempting to parry he replied in quart. The result was that our blades were caught in each other's sleeves; but I had slit his arm, while his point had only pierced the stuff of my coat.

I put myself on guard again to go on, but I could see he was too weak to defend himself, so I said if he liked I would give him quarter.

He made no reply, so I pressed on him, struck him to the ground, and trampled on his body.

He foamed with rage, and told me that it was my turn this time, but that he hoped I would give him his revenge.

"With pleasure, at Rome, and I hope the third lesson will be more effectual than the two I have already given you."

He was losing a good deal of blood, so I sheathed his sword for him and advised him to go to Goudar's house, which was close at hand, and have his wound attended to.

I went back to "Crocielles" as if nothing had happened. The chevalier was making love to Sara, and the rest were playing cards.

I left the company an hour afterwards without having said a word about my duel, and for the last time I supped with Callimena. Six years later I saw her at Venice, displaying her beauty and her talents on the boards of St. Benedict's Theatre.

I spent a delicious night with her, and at eight o'clock the next day I went off in a post-chaise without taking leave of anyone.

I arrived at Salerno at two o'clock in the afternoon, and as soon as I had taken a room I wrote a note to Donna Lucrezia Castelli at the Marquis C——'s.

I asked her if I could pay her a short visit, and begged her to send a reply while I was taking my dinner.

I was sitting down to table when I had the pleasure of seeing Lucrezia herself come in. She gave a cry of delight and rushed to my arms.

This excellent woman was exactly my own age, but she would have been taken for fifteen years younger.

After I had told her how I had come to hear about her I asked for news of our daughter.

"She is longing to see you, and her husband too; he is a worthy old man, and will be so glad to know you."

"How does he know of my existence?"

"Leonilda has mentioned your name a thousand times during the five years they have been married. He is aware that you gave her five thousand ducats. We shall sup together."

"Let us go directly; I cannot rest till I have seen my Leonilda and the good husband God has given her. Have they any children?"

"No, unluckily for her, as after his death the property passes to his relations. But Leonilda will be a rich woman for all that; she will have a hundred thousand ducats of her own."

"You have never married."

"No."

"You are as pretty as you were twenty-six years ago, and if it had not been for the Abbe Galiani I should have left Naples without seeing you."

I found Leonilda had developed into a perfect beauty. She was at that time twenty-three years old.

Her husband's presence was no constraint upon her; she received me with open arms, and put me completely at my ease.

No doubt she was my daughter, but in spite of our relationship and my advancing years I still felt within my breast the symptoms of the tenderest passion for her.

She presented me to her husband, who suffered dreadfully from gout, and could not stir from his arm-chair.

He received me with smiling face and open arms, saying,—

"My dear friend, embrace me."

I embraced him affectionately, and in our greeting I discovered that he was a brother mason. The marquis had expected as much, but I had not; for a nobleman of sixty who could boast that he had been enlightened was a 'rara avis' in the domains of his Sicilian majesty thirty years ago.

I sat down beside him and we embraced each other again, while the ladies looked on amazed, wondering to see us so friendly to each other.

Donna Leonilda fancied that we must be old friends, and told her husband how delighted she was. The old man burst out laughing, and Lucrezia suspecting the truth bit her lips and said nothing. The fair marchioness reserved her curiosity for another reason.

The marquis had seen the whole of Europe. He had only thought of marrying on the death of his father, who had attained the age of ninety. Finding himself in the enjoyment of thirty thousand ducats a year he imagined that he might yet have children in spite of his advanced age. He saw Leonilda, and in a few days he made her his wife, giving her a dowry of a hundred thousand ducats. Donna Lucrezia went to live with her daughter. Though the marquis lived magnificently, he found it difficult to spend more than half his income.

He lodged all his relations in his immense palace; there were three families in all, and each lived apart.

Although they were comfortably off they were awaiting with impatience the death of the head of the family, as they would then share his riches. The marquis had only married in the hope of having an heir; and these hopes he could no longer entertain. However, he loved his wife none the less, while she made him happy by her charming disposition.

The marquis was a man of liberal views like his wife, but this was a great secret, as free thought was not appreciated at Salerno.

Consequently, any outsider would have taken the household for a truly Christian one, and the marquis took care to adopt in appearance all the prejudices of his fellow-countrymen.

Donna Lucrezia told me all this three hours after as we walked in a beautiful garden, where her husband had sent us after a long conversation on subjects which could not have been of any interest to the ladies. Nevertheless, they did not leave us for a moment, so delighted were they to find that the marquis had met a congenial spirit.

About six o'clock the marquis begged Donna Lucrezia to take me to the garden and amuse me till the evening. His wife he asked to stay, as he had something to say to her.

It was in the middle of August and the heat was great, but the room on the ground floor which we occupied was cooled by a delicious breeze.

I looked out of the window and noticed that the leaves on the trees were still, and that no wind was blowing; and I could not help saying to the marquis that I was astonished to find his room as cool as spring in the heats of summer.

"Your sweetheart will explain it to you," said he.

We went through several apartments, and at last reached a closet, in one corner of which was a square opening.

From it rushed a cold and even violent wind. From the opening one could go down a stone staircase of at least a hundred steps, and at the bottom was a grotto where was the source of a stream of water as cold as ice. Donna Lucrezia told me it would be a great risk to go down the steps without excessively warm clothing.

I have never cared to run risks of this kind. Lord Baltimore, on the other hand, would have laughed at the danger, and gone, maybe, to his death. I told my old sweetheart that I could imagine the thing very well from the description, and that I had no curiosity to see whether my imagination were correct.

Lucrezia told me I was very prudent, and took me to the garden.

It was a large place, and separated from the garden common to the three other families who inhabited the castle. Every flower that can be imagined was there, fountains threw their glittering sprays, and grottoes afforded a pleasing shade from the sun.

The alleys of this terrestrial paradise were formed of vines, and the bunches of grapes seemed almost as numerous as the leaves.

Lucrezia enjoyed my surprise, and I told her that I was not astonished at being more moved by this than by the vines of Tivoli and Frascati. The immense rather dazzles the eyes than moves the heart.

She told me that her daughter was happy, and that the marquis was an excellent man, and a strong man except for the gout. His great grief was that he had no children. Amongst his dozen of nephews there was not one worthy of succeeding to the title.

"They are all ugly, awkward lads, more like peasants than noblemen; all their education has been given them by a pack of ignorant priests; and so it is not to be wondered that the marquis does not care for them much."

"But is Leonilda really happy?"

"She is, though her husband cannot be quite so ardent as she would like at her age."

"He doesn't seem to me to be a very jealous man."

"He is entirely free from jealousy, and if Leonilda would take a lover I am sure he would be his best friend. And I feel certain he would be only too glad to find the beautiful soil which he cannot fertile himself fertilized by another."

"Is it positively certain that he is incapable of begetting a child?"

"No, when he is well he does his best; but there seems no likelihood of his ardour having any happy results. There was some ground to hope in the first six months of the marriage, but since he has had the gout so badly there seems reason to fear lest his amorous ecstasies should have a fatal termination. Sometimes he warts to approach her, but she dare not let him, and this pains her very much."

I was struck with a lively sense of Lucrezia's merits, and was just revealing to her the sentiments which she had re-awakened in my breast, when the marchioness appeared in the garden, followed by a page and a young lady.

I affected great reverence as she came up to us; and as if we had given each other the word, she answered me in atone of ceremonious politeness.

"I have come on an affair of the highest importance," she said, "and if I fail I shall for ever lose the reputation of a diplomatist?"

"Who is the other diplomatist with whom you are afraid of failing?"

"'Tis yourself."

"Then your battle is over, for I consent before I know what you ask. I only make a reserve on one point."

"So much the worse, as that may turn out to be just what I want you to do. Tell me what it is."

"I was going to Rome, when the Abbe Galiani told me that Donna Lucrezia was here with you."

"And can a short delay interfere with your happiness? Are you not your own master?"

"Smile on me once more; your desires are orders which must be obeyed. I have always been my own master, but I cease to be so from this moment, since I am your most humble servant."

"Very good. Then I command you to come and spend a few days with us at an estate we have at a short distance. My husband will have himself transported here. You will allow me to send to the inn for your luggage?"

"Here, sweet marchioness, is the key to my room. Happy the mortal whom you deign to command."

Leonilda gave the key to the page, a pretty boy, and told him to see that all my belongings were carefully taken to the castle.

Her lady-in-waiting was very fair. I said so to Leonilda in French, not knowing that the young lady understood the language, but she smiled and told her mistress that we were old acquaintances.

"When had I the pleasure of knowing you, mademoiselle?"

"Nine year ago. You have often spoken to me and teased me."

"Where, may I ask?"

"At the Duchess of Matalone's."

"That may be, and I think I do begin to remember, but I really cannot recollect having teased you."

The marchioness and her mother were highly amused at this conversation, and pressed the girl to say how I had teased her. She confined herself, however, to saying that I had played tricks on her. I thought I remembered having stolen a few kisses, but I left the ladies to think what they liked.

I was a great student of the human heart, and felt that these reproaches of Anastasia's (such was her name) were really advances, but unskillfully made, for if she had wanted more of me, she should have held her peace and bided her time.

"It strikes me," said I, "that you were much smaller in those days."

"Yes, I was only twelve or thirteen. You have changed also."

"Yes, I have aged."

We began talking about the late Duke of Matalone, and Anastasia left us.

We sat down in a charming grotto, and began styling each other papa and daughter, and allowing ourselves liberties which threatened to lead to danger.

The marchioness tried to calm my transports by talking of her good husband.

Donna Lucrezia remarked our mutual emotion as I held Leonilda in my arms, and warned us to be careful. She then left us to walk in a different part of the garden.

Her words had the contrary effect to what was intended, for as soon as she left us in so opportune a manner, although we had no intention of committing the double crime, we approached too near to each other, and an almost involuntary movement made, the act complete.

We remained motionless, looking into one another's eyes, in mute astonishment, as we confessed afterwards, to find neither guilt nor repentance in our breasts.

We rearranged our position, and the marchioness sitting close to me called me her dear husband, while I called her my dear wife.

The new bond between us was confirmed by affectionate kisses. We were absorbed and silent, and Lucrezia was delighted to find us so calm when she returned.

We had no need to warn each other to observe secrecy. Donna Lucrezia was devoid of prejudice, but there was no need to give her a piece of useless information.

We felt certain that she had left us alone, so as not to be a witness of what we were going to do.

After some further conversation we went back to the palace with Anastasia, whom we found in the alley by herself.

The marquis received his wife with joy, congratulating her on the success of her negotiations. He thanked me for my compliance, and assured me I should have a comfortable apartment in his country house.

"I suppose you will not mind having our friend for a neighbor?" he said to Lucrezia.

"No," said she; "but we will be discreet, for the flower of our lives has withered."

"I shall believe as much of that as I please."

The worthy man dearly loved a joke.

The long table was laid for five, and as soon as dinner was served an old priest came in and sat down. He spoke to nobody, and nobody spoke to him.

The pretty page stood behind the marchioness, and we were waited on by ten or twelve servants.

I had only a little soup at dinner, so I ate like an ogre, for I was very hungry, and the marquis's French cook was a thorough artist.

The marquis exclaimed with delight as I devoured one dish after another. He told me that the only fault in his wife that she was a very poor eater like her mother. At dessert the wine began to take effect, and our conversation, which was conducted in French, became somewhat free. The old priest took no notice, as he only understood Italian, and he finally left us after saying the 'agimus'.

The marquis told me that this ecclesiastic had been a confessor to the palace for the last twenty years, but had never confessed anybody. He warned me to take care what I said before him if I spoke Italian, but he did not know a word of French.

Mirth was the order of the day, and I kept the company at table till an hour after midnight.

Before we parted for the night the marquis told me that we would start in the afternoon, and that he should arrive an hour before us. He assured his wife that he was quite well, and that he hoped to convince her that I had made him ten years younger. Leonilda embraced him tenderly, begging him to be careful of his health.

"Yes, yes," said he, "but get ready to receive me."

I wished them a good night, and a little marquis at nine months from date.

"Draw the bill," said he to me, "and to-morrow I will accept it."

"I promise you," said Lucrezia, "to do my best to ensure your meeting your obligations."

Donna Lucrezia took me to my room, where she handed me over to the charge of an imposing-looking servant, and wished me a good night.

I slept for eight hours in a most comfortable bed, and when I was dressed Lucrezia took me to breakfast with the marchioness, who was at her toilette.

"Do you think I may draw my bill at nine months?" said I.

"It will very probably be met," said she.

"Really?"

"Yes, really; and it will be to you that my husband will owe the happiness he has so long desired. He told me so when he left me an hour ago.

"I shall be delighted to add to your mutual happiness."

She looked so fresh and happy that I longed to kiss her, but I was obliged to restrain myself as she was surrounded by her pretty maids.

The better to throw any spies off the scent I began to make love to Anastasia, and Leonilda pretended to encourage me.

I feigned a passionate desire, and I could see that I should not have much trouble in gaining my suit. I saw I should have to be careful if I did not want to be taken at my word; I could not bear such a surfeit of pleasures.

We went to breakfast with the marquis, who was delighted to see us. He was quite well, except the gout which prevented his walking.

After breakfast we heard mass, and I saw about twenty servants in the chapel. After the service I kept the marquis company till dinner-time. He said I was very good to sacrifice the company of the ladies for his sake.

After dinner we set out for his country house; I in a carriage with the two ladies, and the marquis in a litter borne by two mules.

In an hour and a half we arrived at his fine and well-situated castle.

The first thing the marchioness did was to take me into the garden, where my ardour returned and she once more abandoned herself to me.

We agreed that I should only go to her room to court Anastasia, as it was necessary to avoid the slightest suspicion.

This fancy of mine for his wife's maid amused the marquis, for his wife kept him well posted in the progress of our intrigue.

Donna Lucrezia approved of the arrangement as she did not want the marquis to think that I had only come to Salerno for her sake. My apartments were next to Leonilda's, but before I could get into her room I should be obliged to pass through that occupied by Anastasia, who slept with another maid still prettier than herself.

The marquis came an hour later, and he said he would get his people to carry him in an arm-chair round the gardens, so that he might point out their beauties to me. After supper he felt tired and went to bed, leaving me to entertain the ladies.

After a few moments' conversation, I led the marchioness to her room, and she said I had better go to my own apartment through the maids' room, telling Anastasia to shew me the way.

Politeness obliged me to shew myself sensible of such a favour, and I said I hoped she would not be so harsh as to lock her door upon me.

"I shall lock my door," said she, "because it is my duty to do so. This room is my mistress's closet, and my companion would probably make some remark if I left the door open contrary to my usual custom."

"Your reasons are too good for me to overcome, but will you not sit down beside me for a few minutes and help me to recollect how I used to tease you?"

"I don't want you to recollect anything about it; please let me go."

"You must please yourself," said I; and after embracing her and giving her a kiss, I wished her good night.

My servant came in as she went out, and I told him that I would sleep by myself for the future.

The next day the marchioness laughingly repeated the whole of my conversation with Anastasia.

"I applauded her virtuous resistance, but I said she might safely assist at your toilette every evening."

Leonilda gave the marquis a full account of my talk with Anastasia. The old man thought I was really in love with her, and had her in to supper for my sake, so I was in common decency bound to play the lover. Anastasia was highly pleased at my preferring her to her charming mistress, and at the latter's complaisance towards our love-making.

The marquis in his turn was equally pleased as he thought the intrigue would make me stay longer at his house.

In the evening Anastasia accompanied me to my room with a candle, and seeing that I had no valet she insisted combing my hair. She felt flattered at my not presuming to go to bed in her presence, and kept me company for an hour; and as I was not really amorous of her, I had no difficulty in playing the part of the timid lover. When she wished me good night she was delighted to find my kisses as affectionate but not so daring as those of the night before.

The marchioness said, the next morning, that if the recital she had heard were true, she was afraid Anastasia's company tired me, as she very well knew that when I really loved I cast timidity to the winds.

"No, she doesn't tire me at all; she is pretty and amusing. But how can you imagine that I really love her, when you know very well that the whole affair is only designed to cast dust in everyone's eyes?"

"Anastasia fully believes that you adore her, and indeed I am not sorry that you should give her a little taste for gallantry."

"If I can persuade her to leave her door open I can easily visit you, for she will not imagine for a moment that after leaving her I go to your room instead of my own."

"Take care how you set about it."

"I will see what I can do this evening."

The marquis and Lucrezia had not the slightest doubt that Anastasia spent every night with me, and they were delighted at the idea.

The whole of the day I devoted to the worthy marquis, who said my company made him happy. It was no sacrifice on my part, for I liked his principles and his way of thinking.

On the occasion of my third supper with Anastasia I was more tender than ever, and she was very much astonished to find that I had cooled down when I got to my room.

"I am glad to see you so calm," said she, "you quite frightened me at supper."

"The reason is that I know you think yourself in danger when you are alone with me."

"Not at all; you are much more discreet than you were nine years ago."

"What folly did I commit then?"

"No folly, but you did not respect my childhood."

"I only gave you a few caresses, for which I am now sorry, as you are frightened of me, and persist in locking your door."

"I don't mistrust you, but I have told you my reasons for locking the door. I think that you must mistrust me, as you won't go to bed while I am in the room."

"You must think me very presumptuous. I will go to bed, but you must not leave me without giving me a kiss."

"I promise to do so."

I went to bed, and Anastasia spent half an hour beside me. I had a good deal of difficulty in controlling myself, but I was afraid of her telling the marchioness everything.

As she left me she gave me such a kind embrace that I could bear it no longer, and guiding her hand I skewed her the power she exercised over me. She then went away, and I shall not say whether my behaviour irritated or pleased her.

The next day I was curious to know how much she had told the marchioness, and on hearing nothing of the principal fact I felt certain she would not lock her door that evening.

When the evening came I defied her to skew the same confidence in me as I had shewn in her. She replied that she would do so with pleasure, if I would blow out my candle and promise not to put my hand on her. I easily gave her the required promise, for I meant to keep myself fresh for Leonilda.

I undressed hastily, followed her with bare feet, and laid myself beside her.

She took my hands and held them, to which I offered no resistance. We were afraid of awakening her bedfellow, and kept perfect silence. Our lips however gave themselves free course, and certain motions, natural under the circumstances, must have made her believe that I was in torments. The half hour I passed beside her seemed extremely long to me, but it must have been delicious to her, as giving her the idea that she could do what she liked with me.

When I left her after we had shared an ecstatic embrace, I returned to my room, leaving the door open. As soon as I had reason to suppose that she was asleep, I returned, and passed through her room to Leonilda's. She was expecting me, but did not know of my presence till I notified it with a kiss.

After I had given her a strong proof of my love, I told her of my adventure with Anastasia, and then our amorous exploits began again, and I did not leave her till I had spent two most delicious hours. We agreed that they should not be the last, and I returned to my room on tiptoe as I had come.

I did not get up till noon, and the marquis and his wife jested with me at dinner on the subject of my late rising. At supper it was Anastasia's turn, and she seemed to enjoy the situation. She told me in the evening that she would not lock her door, but that I must not come into her room, as it was dangerous. It would be much better, she said, for us to talk in my room, where there would be no need of putting out the light. She added that I had better go to bed, as then she would feel certain that she was not tiring me in any way.

I could not say no, but I flattered myself that I would keep my strength intact for Leonilda.

I reckoned without my host, as the proverb goes.

When I held Anastasia between my arms in bed, her lips glued to mine, I told her, as in duty bound, that she did not trust in me enough to lie beside me with her clothes off.

Thereupon she asked me if I would be very discreet.

If I had said no, I should have looked a fool. I made up my mind, and told her yes, determined to satisfy the pretty girl's desires.

In a moment she was in my arms, not at all inclined to keep me to my promise.

Appetite, it is said, comes in eating. Her ardour made me amorous, and I rendered homage to her charms till I fell asleep with fatigue.

Anastasia left me while I was asleep, and when I awoke I found myself in the somewhat ridiculous position of being obliged to make a full confession to the marchioness as to why I had failed in my duties to her.

When I told Leonilda my tale, she began to laugh and agreed that further visits were out of the question. We made up our minds, and for the remainder of my visit our amorous meetings only took place in the summerhouses in the garden.

I had to receive Anastasia every night, and when I left for Rome and did not take her with me she considered me as a traitor.

The worthy marquis gave me a great surprise on the eve of my departure. We were alone together, and he began by saying that the Duke of Matalone had told him the reason which had prevented me marrying Leonilda, and that he had always admired my generosity in making her a present of five thousand ducats, though I was far from rich.

"These five thousand ducats," he added, "with seven thousand from the duke, composed her dower, and I have added a hundred thousand, so that she is sure of a comfortable living, even if I die without a successor.

"Now, I want you to take back the five thousand ducats you gave her; and she herself is as desirous of your doing so as I am. She did not like to ask you herself; she is too delicate."

"Well, I should have refused Leonilda if she had asked me, but I accept this mark of your friendship. A refusal would have borne witness to nothing but a foolish pride, as I am a poor man. I should like Leonilda and her mother to be present when you give me the money."

"Embrace me; we will do our business after dinner."

Naples has always been a temple of fortune to me, but if I went there   now
I should starve. Fortune flouts old age.

Leonilda and Lucrezia wept with joy when the good marquis gave me the five thousand ducats in bank notes, and presented his mother-in-law with an equal sum in witness of his gratitude to her for having introduced me to him.

The marquis was discreet enough not to reveal his chief reason. Donna
Lucrezia did not know that the Duke of Matalone had told him that
Leonilda was my daughter.

An excess of gratitude lessened my high spirits for the rest of the day, and Anastasia did not spend a very lively night with me.

I went off at eight o'clock the next morning. I was sad, and the whole house was in tears.

I promised that I would write to the marquis from Rome, and I reached
Naples at eleven o'clock.

I went to see Agatha, who was astonished at my appearance as she had thought I was at Rome. Her husband welcomed me in the most friendly manner, although he was suffering a great deal.

I said I would dine with them and start directly afterwards, and I asked the advocate to get me a bill on Rome for five thousand ducats, in exchange for the bank notes I gave him.

Agatha saw that my mind was made up, and without endeavoring to persuade me to stay went in search of Callimena.

She too had thought I was in Rome, and was in an ecstasy of delight to see me again.

My sudden disappearance and my unexpected return were the mystery of the day, but I did not satisfy anyone's curiosity.

I left them at three o'clock, and stopped at Montecasino, which I had never seen. I congratulated myself on my idea, for I met there Prince Xaver de Saxe, who was travelling under the name of Comte de Lusace with Madame Spinucci, a lady of Fermo, with whom he had contracted a semi-clandestine marriage. He had been waiting for three days to hear from the Pope, for by St. Benedict's rule women are not allowed in monasteries; and as Madame Spinucci was extremely curious on the subject, her husband had been obliged to apply for a dispensation to the Holy Father.

I slept at Montecasino after having seen the curiosities of the place, and I went on to Rome, and put up with Roland's daughter in the Place d'Espagne.

CHAPTER XV

Margarita—Madame Buondcorsi—The Duchess of Fiano—Cardinal Bernis—The Princess Santa Croce—Menicuccio and His Sister

I had made up my mind to spend a quiet six months at Rome, and the day after my arrival I took a pleasant suite of rooms opposite the Spanish Ambassador, whose name was d'Aspura. It happened to be the same rooms as were occupied twenty-seven years ago by the teacher of languages, to whom I had gone for lessons while I was with Cardinal Acquaviva. The landlady was the wife of a cook who only, slept with his better half once a week. The woman had a daughter of sixteen or seventeen years old, who would have been very pretty if the small-pox had not deprived her of one eye. They had provided her with an ill-made artificial eye, of a wrong size and a bad colour, which gave a very unpleasant expression to her face. Margarita, as she was called, made no impression on me, but I made her a present which she valued very highly. There was an English oculist named Taylor in Rome at that time, and I got him to make her an eye of the right size and colour. This made Margarita imagine that I had fallen in love with her, and the mother, a devotee, was in some trouble as to whether my intentions were strictly virtuous.

I made arrangements with the mother to supply me with a good dinner and supper without any luxury. I had three thousand sequins, and I had made up my mind to live in a quiet and respectable manner.

The next day I found letters for me in several post-offices, and the banker Belloni, who had known me for several years, had been already advised of my bill of exchange. My good friend Dandolo sent me two letters of introduction, of which one was addressed to M. Erizzo, the Venetian ambassador. He was the brother of the ambassador to Paris. This letter pleased me greatly. The other was addressed to the Duchess of Fiano, by her brother M. Zuliani.

I saw that I should be free of all the best houses, and I promised myself the pleasure of an early visit to Cardinal Bernis.

I did not hire either a carriage or a servant. At Rome both these articles are procurable at a moment's notice.

My first call was on the Duchess of Fiano. She was an ugly woman, and though she was really very good-natured, she assumed the character of being malicious so as to obtain some consideration.

Her husband, who bore the name of Ottoboni, had only married her to obtain an heir, but the poor devil turned out to be what the Romans call 'babilano', and we impotent. The duchess told me as much on the occasion of my third visit. She did not give me the information in a complaining tone, or as if she was fain to be consoled, but merely to defy her confessor, who had threatened her with excommunication if she went on telling people about her husband's condition, or if she tried to cure him of it.

The duchess gave a little supper every evening to her select circle of friends. I was not admitted to these reunions for a week or ten days, by which time I had made myself generally popular. The duke did not care for company and supped apart.

The Prince of Santa Croce was the duchess's 'cavaliere servante', and the princess was served by Cardinal Bernis. The princess was a daughter of the Marquis Falconieri, and was young, pretty, lively, and intended by nature for a life of pleasure. However, her pride at possessing the cardinal was so great that she did not give any hope to other competitors for her favour.

The prince was a fine man of distinguished manners and great capability, which he employed in business speculations, being of opinion, and rightly, that it was no shame for a nobleman to increase his fortune by the exercise of his intelligence. He was a careful man, and had attached himself to the duchess because she cost him nothing, and he ran no risk of falling in love with her.

Two or three weeks after my arrival he heard me complaining of the obstacles to research in the Roman libraries, and he offered to give me an introduction to the Superior of the Jesuits. I accepted the offer, and was made free of the library; I could not only go and read when I liked, but I could, on writing my name down, take books away with me. The keepers of the library always brought me candles when it grew dark, and their politeness was so great that they gave me the key of a side door, so that I could slip in and out as I pleased.

The Jesuits were always the most polite of the regular clergy, or, indeed, I may say the only polite men amongst them; but during the crisis in which they were then involved, they were simply cringing.

The King of Spain had called for the suppression of the order, and the Pope had promised that it should be done; but the Jesuits did not think that such a blow could ever be struck, and felt almost secure. They did not think that the Pope's power was superhuman so far as they were concerned. They even intimated to him by indirect channels that his authority did not extend to the suppression of the order; but they were mistaken. The sovereign pontiff delayed the signature of the bull, but his hesitation proceeded from the fact that in signing it he feared lest he should be signing his own sentence of death. Accordingly he put it off till he found that his honour was threatened. The King of Spain, the most obstinate tyrant in Europe, wrote to him with his own hand, telling him that if he did not suppress the order he would publish in all the languages of Europe the letters he had written when he was a cardinal, promising to suppress the order when he became Pope. On the strength of these letters Ganganelli had been elected.

Another man would have taken refuge in casuistry and told the king that it was not for a pope to be bound to the cardinal's promises, in which contention he would have been supported by the Jesuits. However, in his heart Ganganelli had no liking for the Jesuits. He was a Franciscan, and not a gentleman by birth. He had not a strong enough intellect to defy the king and all his threats, or to bear the shame of being exhibited to the whole world as an ambitious and unscrupulous man.

I am amused when people tell me that Ganganelli poisoned himself by taking so many antidotes. It is true that having reason, and good reason, to dread poison, he made use of antidotes which, with his ignorance of science, might have injured his health; but I am morally certain that he died of poison which was given by other hands than his own.

My reasons for this opinion are as follows:

In the year of which I am speaking, the third of the Pontificate of Clement XIV., a woman of Viterbo was put in prison on the charge of making predictions. She obscurely prophesied the suppression of the Jesuits, without giving any indication of the time; but she said very clearly that the company would be destroyed by a pope who would only reign five years three months and three days—that is, as long as Sixtus V., not a day more and not a day less.

Everybody treated the prediction with contempt, as the product of a brain-sick woman. She was shut up and quite forgotten.

I ask my readers to give a dispassionate judgment, and to say whether they have any doubt as to the poisoning of Ganganelli when they hear that his death verified the prophecy.

In a case like this, moral certainty assumes the force of scientific certainty. The spirit which inspired the Pythia of Viterbo took its measures to inform the world that if the Jesuits were forced to submit to being suppressed, they were not so weak as to forego a fearful vengeance. The Jesuit who cut short Ganganelli's days might certainly have poisoned him before the bull was signed, but the fact was that they could not bring themselves to believe it till it took place. It is clear that if the Pope had not suppressed the Jesuits, they would not have poisoned him, and here again the prophecy could not be taxed with falsity. We may note that Clement XIV., like Sixtus V., was a Franciscan, and both were of low birth. It is also noteworthy that after the Pope's death the prophetess was liberated, and, though her prophecy had been fulfilled to the letter, all the authorities persisted in saying that His Holiness had died from his excessive use of antidotes.

It seems to me that any impartial judge will scout the idea of Ganganelli having killed himself to verify the woman of Viterbo's prediction. If you say it was a mere coincidence, of course I cannot absolutely deny your position, for it may have been chance; but my thoughts on the subject will remain unchanged.

This poisoning was the last sign the Jesuits gave of their power. It was a crime, because it was committed after the event, whereas, if it had been done before the suppression of the order, it would have been a stroke of policy, and might have been justified on politic grounds. The true politician looks into the future, and takes swift and certain measures to obtain the end he has in view.

The second time that the Prince of Santa Croce saw me at the Duchess of Fiano's, he asked me 'ex abrupta' why I did not visit Cardinal Bernis.

"I think of paying my suit to him to-morrow," said I.

"Do so, for I have never heard his eminence speak of anyone with as much consideration as he speaks of yourself."

"He has been very kind to me, and I shall always be grateful to him."

The cardinal received me the next day with every sign of delight at seeing me. He praised the reserve with which I had spoken of him to the prince, and said he need not remind me of the necessity for discretion as to our old Venetian adventures.

"Your eminence," I said, "is a little stouter, otherwise you look as fresh as ever and not at all changed."

"You make a mistake. I am very different from what I was then. I am fifty-five now, and then I was thirty-six. Moreover, I am reduced to a vegetable diet."

"Is that to keep down the lusts of the flesh?"

"I wish people would think so; but no one does, I am afraid."

He was glad to hear that I bore a letter to the Venetian ambassador, which I had not yet presented. He said he would take care to give the ambassador a prejudice in my favour, and that he would give me a good reception.

"We will begin to break the ice to-morrow," added this charming cardinal.
"You shall dine with me, and his excellence shall hear of it."

He heard with pleasure that I was well provided for as far as money was concerned, and that I had made up my mind to live simply and discreetly so long as I remained in Rome.

"I shall write about you to M—— M——," he said. "I have always kept up a correspondence with that delightful nun."

I then amused him by the talk of my adventure with the nun of Chamberi.

"You ought to ask the Prince of Santa Croce to introduce you to the princess. We might pass some pleasant hours with her, though not in our old Venetian style, for the princess is not at all like M—— M——.

"And yet she serves to amuse your eminence?"

"Well, I have to be content with what I can get."

The next day as I was getting up from dinner the cardinal told me that M. Zuliani had written about me to the ambassador, who would be delighted to make my acquaintance, and when I went I had an excellent reception from him.

The Chevalier Erizzo, who is still alive, was a man of great intelligence, common sense, and oratorical power. He complimented me on my travels and on my being protected by the State Inquisitors instead of being persecuted by them. He kept me to dinner, and asked me to dine with him whenever I had no other engagement.

The same evening I met Prince Santa Croce at the duchess's, and asked him to introduce me to his wife.

"I have been expecting that," he replied "even since the cardinal talked to her about you for more than an hour. You can call any day at eleven in the morning or two in the afternoon."

I called the next day at two o'clock. She was taking her siesta in bed, but as I had the privileges allowed to a person of no consequence she let me in directly. She was young, pretty, lively, curious, and talkative; she had not enough patience to wait for my answer to her questions. She struck me as a toy, well adapted to amuse a man of affairs, who felt the need of some distraction. The cardinal saw her regularly three times a day; the first thing in the morning he called to ask if she had had a good night, at three o'clock in the afternoon he took coffee with her, and in the evening he met her at the assembly. He always played at piquet, and played with such talent that he invariably lost six Roman sequins, no more and no less. These losses of the cardinal's made the princess the richest young wife in Rome.

Although the marquis was somewhat inclined to be jealous, he could not possibly object to his wife enjoying a revenue of eighteen hundred francs a month, and that without the least scandal, for everything was done in public, and the game was honestly conducted. Why should not fortune fall in love with such a pretty woman?

The Prince of Santa Croce could not fail to appreciate the friendship of the cardinal for his wife, who gave him a child every year, and sometimes every nine months, in spite of the doctor's warnings to beware of results. It was said that to make up for his enforced abstinence during the last few days of his wife's pregnancy, the prince immediately set to again when the child was being baptized.

The friendship of the cardinal for the prince's wife also gave him the advantage of getting silks from Lyons without the Pope's treasurer being able to say anything, as the packets were addressed to the French ambassador. It must also be noted that the cardinal's patronage kept other lovers from the house. The High Constable Colonna was very much taken with her. The prince had surprised this gentleman talking to the princess in a room of the palace and at an hour when she was certain that the cardinal would not be in the way. Scarcely had the Colonna gone when the prince told his wife that she would accompany him into the country the next day. She protested, saying that this sudden order was only a caprice and that her honour would not allow of her obeying him. The prince, however, was very determined, and she would have been obliged to go if the cardinal had not come in and heard the story from the mouth of the innocent princess. He shewed the husband that it was to his own interests to go into the country by himself, and to let his wife remain in Rome. He spoke for her, assuring the prince that she would take more care for the future and avoid such meetings, always unpleasant in a house.

In less than a month I became the shadow of the three principal persons in the play. I listened and admired and became as necessary to the personages as a marker at billiards. When any of the parties were afflicted I consoled them with tales or amusing comments, and, naturally, they were grateful to me. The cardinal, the prince, and his fair wife amused each other and offended no one.

The Duchess of Fiano was proud of being the possessor of the prince who left his wife to the cardinal, but no one was deceived but herself. The good lady wondered why no one acknowledged that the reason why the princess never came to see her was mere jealousy. She spoke to me on the subject with so much fire that I had to suppress my good sense to keep her good graces.

I had to express my astonishment as to what the cardinal could see in the princess, who, according to her, was skinny in person and silly in mind, altogether a woman of no consequence. I agreed to all this, but I was far from thinking so, for the princess was just the woman to amuse a voluptuous and philosophic lover like the cardinal.

I could not help thinking now and again that the cardinal was happier in the possession of this treasure of a woman than in his honours and dignities.

I loved the princess, but as I did not hope for success I confined myself strictly to the limits of my position.

I might, no doubt, have succeeded, but more probably I should have raised her pride against me, and wounded the feelings of the cardinal, who was no longer the same as when we shared M——M—— in common. He had told me that his affection for her was of a purely fatherly character, and I took that as a hint not to trespass on his preserves.

I had reason to congratulate myself that she observed no more ceremony with me than with her mail. I accordingly pretended to see nothing, while she felt certain I saw all.

It is no easy matter to win the confidence of such a woman, especially if she be served by a king or a cardinal.

My life at Rome was a tranquil and happy one. Margarita had contrived to gain my interest by the assiduity of her attentions. I had no servant, so she waited on me night and morning, and her false eye was such an excellent match that I quite forgot its falsity. She was a clever, but a vain girl, and though at first I had no designs upon her I flattered her vanity by my conversation and the little presents I bestowed upon her, which enabled her to cut a figure in church on Sundays. So before long I had my eyes opened to two facts; the one that she was sure of my love, and wondered why I did not declare it; the other, that if I chose I had an easy conquest before me.

I guessed the latter circumstance one day when, after I had asked her to tell me her adventures from the age of eleven to that of eighteen, she proceeded to tell me tales, the telling of which necessitated her throwing all modesty to the winds.

I took the utmost delight in these scandalous narrations, and whenever I thought she had told the whole truth I gave her a few pieces of money; while whenever I had reason to suppose that she had suppressed some interesting circumstances I gave her nothing.

She confessed to me that she no longer possessed that which a maid can lose but once, that a friend of hers named Buonacorsi was in the same case, and finally she told me the name of the young man who had relieved them both of their maidenheads.

We had for neighbor a young Piedmontese abbe named Ceruti, on whom Margarita was obliged to wait when her mother was too busy. I jested with her about him, but she swore there was no lovemaking between them.

This abbe was a fine man, learned and witty, but he was overwhelmed with debt and in very bad odour at Rome on account of an extremely unpleasant story of which he was the hero.

They said that he had told an Englishman, who was in love with Princess Lanti, that she was in want of two hundred sequins, that the Englishman had handed over the money to the abbe, and that the latter had appropriated it.

This act of meanness had been brought to light by an explanation between the lady and the Englishman. On his saying to the princess that he was ready to do anything for her, and that the two hundred sequins he had given her were as nothing in comparison with what he was ready to do, she indignantly denied all knowledge of the transaction. Everything came out. The Englishman begged pardon, and the abbe was excluded from the princess's house and the Englishman's also.

This Abbe Ceruti was one of those journalists employed to write the weekly news of Rome by Bianconi; he and I had in a manner become friends since we were neighbours. I saw that he loved Margarita, and I was not in the least jealous, but as he was a handsome young fellow I could not believe that Margarita was cruel to him. Nevertheless, she assured me that she detested him, and that she was very sorry that her mother made her wait on him at all.

Ceruti had already laid himself under obligations to me. He had borrowed a score of crowns from me, promising to repay them in a week, and three weeks had gone by without my seeing the money. However, I did not ask for it, and would have lent him as much more if he had requested me. But I must tell the story as it happened.

Whenever I supped with the Duchess of Fiano I came in late, and Margarita waited up for me. Her mother would go to bed. For the sake of amusement I used to keep her for an hour or two without caring whether our pleasantries disturbed the abbe, who could hear everything we said.

One evening I came home at midnight and was surprised to find the mother waiting for me.

"Where is your daughter?" I enquired.

"She's asleep, and I really cannot allow you to pass the whole night with her any longer."

"But she only stays with me till I get into bed. This new whim wounds my feelings. I object to such unworthy suspicions. What has Margarita been telling you? If she has made any complaints of me, she has lied, and I shall leave your house to-morrow."

"You are wrong; Margarita has made no complaints; on the contrary she says that you have done nothing to her."

"Very good. Do you think there is any harm in a little joking?"

"No, but you might be better employed."

"And these are your grounds for a suspicion of which you should be ashamed, if you are a good Christian."

"God save me from thinking evil of my neighbour, but I have been informed that your laughter and your jests are of such a nature as to be offensive to people of morality."

"Then it is my neighbour the abbe who has been foolish enough to give you this information?"

"I cannot tell you how I heard it, but I have heard it."

"Very good. To-morrow I shall seek another lodging, so as to afford your tender conscience some relief."

"Can't I attend on you as well as my daughter?"

"No; your daughter makes me laugh, and laughing is beneficial to me, whereas you would not make me laugh at all. You have insulted me, and I leave your house to-morrow."

"I shall have to tell my husband the reason of your departure, and I do not want to do that."

"You can do as you like; that's no business of mine. Go away; I want to get into bed."

"Allow me to wait on you."

"Certainly not; if you want anybody to wait on me, send Margarita."

"She's asleep."

"Then wake her up."

The good woman went her way, and two minutes later, the girl came in with little on but her chemise. She had not had time to put in her false eye, and her expression was so amusing that I went off into a roar of laughter.

"I was sleeping soundly," she began, "and my mother woke me up all of a sudden, and told me to come and wait on you, or else you would leave, and my father would think we had been in mischief."

"I will stay, if you will continue to wait on me."

"I should like to come very much, but we mustn't laugh any more, as the abbe has complained of us."

"Oh! it is the abbe, is it?"

"Of course it is. Our jests and laughter irritate his passions."

"The rascal! We will punish him rarely. If we laughed last night, we will laugh ten times louder tonight."

Thereupon we began a thousand tricks, accompanied by shouts and shrieks of laughter, purposely calculated to drive the little priest desperate. When the fun was at its height, the door opened and the mother came in.

I had Margarita's night-cap on my head, and Margarita's face was adorned with two huge moustaches, which I had stuck on with ink. Her mother had probably anticipated taking us in the fact, but when she came in she was obliged to re-echo our shouts of mirth.

"Come now," said I, "do you think our amusements criminal?"

"Not a bit; but you see your innocent orgies keep your neighbour awake."

"Then he had better go and sleep somewhere else; I am not going to put myself out for him. I will even say that you must choose between him and me; if I consent to stay with you, you must send him away, and I will take his room."

"I can't send him away before the end of the month, and I am afraid he will say things to my husband which will disturb the peace of the house."

"I promise you he shall go to-morrow and say nothing at all. Leave him to me; the abbe shall leave of his own free will, without giving you the slightest trouble. In future be afraid for your daughter when she is alone with a man and you don't hear laughing. When one does not laugh, one does something serious."

After this the mother seemed satisfied and went off to bed. Margarita was in such high spirits over the promised dismissal of the abbe that I could not resist doing her justice. We passed an hour together without laughing, and she left me very proud of the victory she had gained.

Early the next day I paid the abbe a visit, and after reproaching him for his behaviour I gave him his choice between paying me the money he owed me and leaving the house at once. He did his best to get out of the dilemma, but seeing that I was pitiless he said he could not leave without paying a few small sums he owed the landlord, and without the wherewithal to obtain another lodging.

"Very good," said I, "I will present you with another twenty crowns; but you must go to-day, and not say a word to anyone, unless you wish me to become your implacable enemy."

I thus got rid of him and entered into possession of the two rooms. Margarita was always at my disposal, and after a few days so was the fair Buonacorsi, who was much the prettier of the two.

The two girls introduced me to the young man who had seduced them.

He was a lad of fifteen or sixteen, and very handsome though short. Nature had endowed him with an enormous symbol of virility, and at Lampsacus he would no doubt have had an altar erected to him beside that of Priapus, with which divinity he might well have contended.

He was well-mannered and agreeable, and seemed much above a common workman. He did not love Margarita or Mdlle. Bounacorsi; he had merely satisfied their curiosity. They saw and admired, and wished to come to a nearer acquaintance; he read their minds and offered to satisfy them. Thereupon the two girls held a consultation, and pretending to submit out of mere complaisance; the double deed was done. I liked this young man, and gave him linen and clothes. So before long he had complete confidence in me. He told me he was in love with a girl, but unhappily for him she was in a convent, and not being able to win her he was becoming desperate. The chief obstacle to the match lay in the fact that his earnings only amounted to a paul a day, which was certainly an insufficient sum to support a wife on.

He talked so much about her that I became curious, and expressed a desire to see her. But before coming to this I must recite some other incidents of my stay at Rome.

One day I went to the Capitol to see the prizes given to the art students, and the first face I saw was the face of Mengs. He was with Battoni and two or three other painters, all being occupied in adjudging the merits of the various pictures.

I had not forgotten his treatment of me at Madrid, so I pretended not to see him; but as soon as he saw me, he came up and addressed me as follows:

"My dear Casanova, let us forget what happened at Madrid and be friends once more."

"So be it, provided no allusion is made to the cause of our quarrel; for
I warn you that I cannot speak of it and keep my head cool."

"I dare say; but if you had understood my position at Madrid you would never have obliged me to take a course which gave me great pain."

"I do not understand you."

"I dare say not. You must know, then, that I was strongly suspected of being a Protestant; and if I had shewn myself indifferent to your conduct, I might possibly have been ruined. But dine with me tomorrow; we will make up a party of friends, and discuss our quarrel in a good bottle of wine. I know that you do not receive your brother, so he shall not be there. Indeed, I do not receive him myself, for if I did all honest people would give me the cold shoulder."

I accepted his friendly invitation, and was punctual to the appointment.

My brother left Rome a short time afterwards with Prince Beloselski, the Russian ambassador to Dresden, with whom he had come; but his visit was unsuccessful, as Rezzonico proved inexorable. We only saw each other two or three times at Rome.

Three or four days after he had gone I had the agreeable surprise of seeing my brother the priest, in rags as usual. He had the impudence to ask me to help him.

"Where do you come from?"

"From Venice; I had to leave the place, as I could no longer make a living there."

"Then how do you think of making a living at Rome?"

"By saying masses and teaching French."

"You a teacher of languages! Why, you do not know your native tongue."

"I know Italian and French too, and I have already got two pupils."

"They will no doubt make wonderful progress under your fostering   care.
Who are they?"

"The son and daughter of the inn-keeper, at whose house I am staying. But that's not enough to keep me, and you must give me something while I am starting."

"You have no right to count on me. Leave the room."

I would not listen to another word, and told Margarita to see that he did not come in again.

The wretched fellow did his best to ruin me with all my friends, including the Duchess of Fiano and the Abbe Gama. Everybody told me that I should either give him some help, or get him out of Rome; I got heartily sick of the sound of his name. At last the Abbe Ceruti came and told me that if I did not want to see my brother begging his bread in the streets I must give him some assistance.

"You can keep him out of Rome," he said, "and he is ready to go if you will allow him three pauls a day." I consented, and Ceruti hit on a plan which pleased me very much. He spoke to a priest who served a convent of Franciscan nuns. This priest took my brother into his service, and gave him three pauls for saying one mass every day. If he could preach well he might earn more.

Thus the Abbe Casanova passed away, and I did not care whether he knew or not where the three pauls had come from. As long as I stayed at Rome the nine piastres a month came in regularly, but after my departure he returned to Rome, went to another convent, and died there suddenly thirteen or fourteen years ago.

Medini had also arrived in Rome, but we had not seen each other. He lived in the street of the Ursulines at the house of one of the Pope's light-cavalry men, and subsisted on the money he cheated strangers of.

The rascal had done well and had sent to Mantua for his mistress, who came with her mother and a very pretty girl of twelve or thirteen. Thinking it would be to his advantage to take handsome furnished apartments he moved to the Place d'Espagne, and occupied a house four or five doors from me, but I knew nothing of all this at the time.

Happening to dine one day with the Venetian ambassador, his excellency told me that I should meet a certain Count. Manucci who had just arrived from Paris, and had evinced much delight on learning that I was at Rome.

"I suppose you know him well," said the ambassador, "and as I am going to present him to the Holy Father to-morrow, I should be much obliged if you could tell me who he really is."

"I knew him at Madrid, where he lived with Mocenigo our ambassador; he is well mannered, polite, and a fine looking young man, and that's all I know about him."

"Was he received at the Spanish Court?"

"I think so, but I cannot be positive."

"Well, I think he was not received; but I see that you won't tell me all you know about him. It's of no consequence; I shall run no risk in presenting him to the Pope. He says he is descended from Manucci, the famous traveller of the thirteenth century, and from the celebrated printers of the same name who did so much for literature. He shewed me the Aldine anchor on his coat of arms which has sixteen quarters."

I was astonished beyond measure that this man who had plotted my assassination should speak of me as an intimate friend, and I determined to conceal my feelings and await events. I did not shew the least sign of anger, and when after greeting the ambassador he came up to me with open arms, I received him cordially and asked after Mocenigo.

Manucci talked a great deal at dinner, telling a score of lies, all in my honour, about my reception at Madrid. I believe his object was to force me to lie too, and to make me do the same for him another time.

I swallowed all these bitter pills, for I had no choice in the matter, but I made up my mind I would have a thorough explanation the next day.

A Frenchman, the Chevalier de Neuville by name, who had come with
Manucci, interested me a great deal. He had come to Rome to

endeavour to

obtain the annulment of marriage of a lady who was in a convent at

Mantua. He had a special recommendation to Cardinal Galli.

His conversation was particularly agreeable, and when we left the ambassador's I accepted the offer to come into his carriage with Manucci, and we drove about till the evening.

As we were returning at nightfall he told us that he was going to present us to a pretty girl with whom we would sup and where we should have a game of faro.

The carriage stopped at the Place d'Espagne, at a short distance from my lodging, and we went up to a room on the second floor. When I went in I was surprised to see Count Medini and his mistress, the lady whom the chevalier had praised, and whom I found not at all to my taste. Medini received me cordially, and thanked the Frenchman for having made me forget the past, and having brought me to see him.

M. de Neuville looked astonished, and to avoid any unpleasant explanations I turned the conversation.

When Medini thought a sufficient number of punters were present he sat down at a large table, placed five or six hundred crowns in gold and notes before him, and began to deal. Manucci lost all the gold he had about him, Neuville swept away half the bank, and I was content with the humble part of spectator.

After supper, Medini asked the chevalier to give him his revenge, and Manucci asked me to lend him a hundred sequins. I did so, and in an hour he had not one left. Neuville, on the other hand, brought down Medini's bank to twenty or thirty sequins, and after that we retired to our several homes.

Manucci lodged with my sister-in-law, Roland's daughter, and I had made up my mind to give him an early call; but he did not leave me the opportunity, as he called on me early in the morning.

After returning me the hundred sequins he embraced me affectionately, and, shewing me a large letter of credit on Bettoni, said that I must consider his purse as mine. In short, though he said nothing about the past, he gave me to understand that he wished to initiate a mutual policy of forget and forgive.

On this occasion my heart proved too strong for my brain; such has often been the case with me. I agreed to the articles of peace he offered and required.

Besides, I was no longer at that headstrong age which only knows one kind of satisfaction, that of the sword. I remembered that if Manucci had been wrong so had I, and I felt that my honour ran no danger of being compromised.

The day after, I went to dinner with him. The Chevalier de Neuville came in towards the close of the meal, and Medini a few moments later. The latter called on us to hold a bank, each in his turn, and we agreed. Manucci gained double what he had lost; Neuville lost four hundred sequins, and I only lost a trifle. Medini who had only lost about fifty sequins was desperate, and would have thrown himself out of the window.

A few days later Manucci set out for Naples, after giving a hundred louis to Medini's mistress, who used to sup with him; but this windfall did not save Medini from being imprisoned for debt, his liabilities amounting to more than a thousand crowns.

The poor wretch wrote me doleful epistles, entreating me to come to his assistance; but the sole effect of his letters was to make me look after what he called his family, repaying myself with the enjoyment of his mistress's young sister. I did not feel called upon to behave generously to him for nothing.

About this time the Emperor of Germany came to Rome with his brother, the Grand Duke of Tuscany.

One of the noblemen in their suite made the girl's acquaintance, and gave Medini enough to satisfy his creditors. He left Rome soon after recovering his liberty, and we shall meet him again in a few months.

I lived very happily amongst the friends I had made for myself. In the evenings I visited the Duchess of Fiano, in the afternoons the Princess of Santa Croce. The rest of my time I spent at home, where I had Margarita, the fair Buonacorsi, and young Menicuccio, who told me so much about his lady-love that I felt quite curious to see her.

The girl was in a kind of convent where she had been placed out of charity. She could only leave it to get married, with the consent of the cardinal who superintended the establishment. When a girl went out and got married, she received a dower of two hundred Roman crowns.

Menicuccio had a sister in the same convent, and was allowed to visit her on Sundays; she came to the grating, followed by her governess. Though Menicuccio was her brother, she was not permitted to see him alone.

Five or six months before the date of which I am writing his sister had been accompanied to the grating by another girl, whom he had never seen before, and he immediately fell in love with her.

The poor young man had to work hard all the week, and could only visit the convent on holidays; and even then he had rarely the good luck to see his lady-love. In five or six months he had only seen her seven or eight times.

His sister knew of his love, and would have done all in her power for him, but the choice of a companion did not rest with her, and she was afraid of asking for this particular girl for fear of exciting suspicion.

As I have said, I had made up my mind to pay the place a visit, and on our way Menicuccio told me that the women of the convent were not nuns, properly speaking, as they had never taken any vow and did not wear a monastic dress. In spite of that they had few temptations to leave their prison house, as they would only find themselves alone in the world with the prospect of starvation or hard work before them. The young girls only came out to get married, which was uncommon, or by flight, which was extremely difficult.

We reached a vast ill-built house, near one of the town gates—a lonely and deserted situation, as the gate led to no highway. When we went into the parlour I was astonished to see the double grating with bars so thick and close together that the hand of a girl of ten could scarce have got through. The grating was so close that it was extremely difficult to make out the features of the persons standing on the inner side, especially as this was only lighted by the uncertain reflection from the outer room. The sight of these arrangements made me shudder.

"How and where have you seen your mistress?" I asked Menicuccio; "for there I see nothing but darkness."

"The first time the governess chanced to have a candle, but this privilege is confined, under pain of excommunication, to relations."

"Then she will have a light to-day?"

"I expect not, as the portress will have sent up word that there was a stranger with me."

"But how could you see your sweetheart, as you are not related to her?"

"By chance; the first time she came my sister's governess—a good soul—said nothing about it. Ever since there has been no candle when she has been present." Soon after, the forms of three or four women were dimly to be seen; but there was no candle, and the governess would not bring one on any consideration. She was afraid of being found out and excommunicated.

I saw that I was depriving my young friend of a pleasure, and would have gone, but he told me to stay. I passed an hour which interested me in spite of its painfulness. The voice of Menicuccio's sister sent a thrill through me, and I fancied that the blind must fall in love through their sense of hearing. The governess was a woman under thirty. She told me that when the girls attained their twenty-fifth year they were placed in charge of the younger ones, and at thirty-five they were free to leave the convent if they liked, but that few cared to take this step, for fear of falling into misery.

"Then there are a good many old women here?"

"There are a hundred of us, and the number is only decreased by death and by occasional marriages."

"But how do those who go out to get married succeed in inspiring the love of their husbands?"

"I have been here for twenty years, and in that time only four have gone out, and they did not know their husbands till they met at the altar. As might be expected, the men who solicit the cardinal for our hands are either madmen, or fellows of desperate fortunes who want the two hundred piastres. However, the cardinal-superintendent refuses permission unless the postulant can satisfy him that he is capable of supporting a wife."

"How does he choose his bride?"

"He tells the cardinal what age and disposition he would prefer, and the cardinal informs the mother-superior."

"I suppose you keep a good table, and are comfortably lodged."

"Not at all. Three thousand crowns a year are not much to keep a hundred persons. Those who do a little work and earn something are the best off."

"What manner of people put their daughters in such a prison?"

"Either poor people or bigots who are afraid of their children falling into evil ways. We only receive pretty girls here."

"Who is the judge of their prettiness?"

"The parents, the priest, and on the last appeal the cardinal-superintendent, who rejects plain girls without pity, observing that ugly women have no reason to fear the seductions of vice. So you may imagine that, wretched as we are, we curse those who pronounced us pretty."

"I pity you, and I wonder why leave is not given to see you openly; you might have some chance of getting married then."

"The cardinal says that it is not in his power to give permission, as anyone transgressing the foundation is excommunicated."

"Then I should imagine that the founder of this house is now consumed by the flames of hell."

"We all think so, and hope he may stay there. The Pope ought to take some order with the house."

I gave her ten crowns, saying that as I could not see her I could not promise a second visit, and then I went away with Menicuccio, who was angry with himself for having procured me such a tedious hour.

"I suppose I shall never see your mistress or your sister," said I; "your sister's voice went to my heart."

"I should think your ten paistres ought to work miracles."

"I suppose there is another parlour."

"Yes; but only priests are allowed to enter it under pain of excommunication, unless you get leave from the Holy Father."

I could not imagine how such a monstrous establishment could be tolerated, for it was almost impossible, under the circumstances, for the poor girls to get a husband. I calculated that as two hundred piastres were assigned to each as a dowry in case of marriage, the founder must have calculated on two marriages a year at least, and it seemed probable that these sums were made away with by some scoundrel.

I laid my ideas before Cardinal Bernis in the presence of the princess, who seemed moved with compassion for these poor women, and said I must write out a petition and get it signed by all of them, entreating the Holy Father to allow them the privileges customary in all other convents.

The cardinal told me to draft the supplication, to obtain the signatures, and to place it in the hands of the princess. In the meantime he would get the ear of the Holy Father, and ascertain by whose hands it was most proper for the petition to be presented.

I felt pretty sure of the signatures of the greater number of the recluses, and after writing out the petition I left it in the hands of the governess to whom I had spoken before. She was delighted with the idea, and promised to give me back the paper when I came again, with the signatures of all her companions in misfortune.

As soon as the Princess Santa Croce had the document she addressed herself to the Cardinal-Superintendent Orsini, who promised to bring the matter before the Pope. Cardinal Bernis had already spoken to His Holiness.

The chaplain of the institute was ordered to warn the superior that for the future visitors were to be allowed to see girls in the large parlour, provided they were accompanied by a governess.

Menicuccio brought me this news, which the princess had not heard, and which she was delighted to hear from my lips.

The worthy Pope did not stop there. He ordered a rigid scrutiny of the accounts to be made, and reduced the number from a hundred to fifty, doubling the dower. He also ordered that all girls who reached the age of twenty-five without getting married should be sent away with their four hundred crowns apiece; that twelve discreet matrons should have charge of the younger girls, and that twelve servants should be paid to do the hard work of the house.

CHAPTER XVI

I Sup at the Inn With Armelline and Emilie

These innovations were the work of some six months. The first reform was the abolition of the prohibition on entering the large parlour and even the interior of the convent; for as the inmates had taken no vows and were not cloistered nuns, the superior should have been at liberty to act according to her discretion. Menicuccio had learnt this from a note his sister wrote him, and which he brought to me in high glee, asking me to come with him to the convent, according to his sister's request, who said my presence would be acceptable to her governess. I was to ask for the governess.

I was only too glad to lend myself to this pleasant arrangement, and felt curious to see the faces of the three recluses, as well as to hear what they had to say on these great changes.

When we got into the large parlour I saw two grates, one occupied by the Abbe Guasco, whom I had known in Paris in 1751, the other by a Russian nobleman, Ivan Ivanovitch Schuvaloff, and by Father Jacquier, a friar minim of the Trinita dei Monti, and a learned astronomer. Behind the grate I saw three very pretty girls.

When our friends came down we began a very interesting conversation, which had to be conducted in a low tone for fear of our being overheard. We could not talk at our ease till the other visitors had taken their leave. My young friend's mistress was a very pretty girl, but his sister was a ravishing beauty. She had just entered on her sixteenth year, but she was tall and her figure well developed; in short, she enchanted me. I thought I had never seen a whiter skin or blacker hair and eyebrows and eyes, but still more charming was the sweetness of her voice and expression, and the naïve simplicity of her expressions. Her governess who was ten or twelve years older than she was, was a woman of an extremely interesting expression; she was pale and melancholy looking, no doubt from the fires which she had been forced to quench within her. She delighted me by telling me of the confusion which the new regulations had caused in the house.

"The mother-superior is well pleased," she said, "and all my young companions are overjoyed; but the older ones whom circumstance has made into bigots are scandalized at everything. The superior has already given orders for windows to be made in the dark parlours, though the old women say that she cannot go beyond the concessions she has already received. To this the superior answered that as free communication had been allowed, it would be absurd to retain the darkness. She has also given orders for the alteration of the double grating, as there was only a single one in the large parlour."

I thought the superior must be a woman of intelligence, and expressed a desire to see her. Emilie obtained this pleasure for me the following day.

Emilie was the friend of Armelline, Menicuccio's sister. This first visit lasted two hours, and seemed all too short. Menicuccio spoke to his well-beloved at the other grating.

I went away, after having given them ten Roman crowns as before. I kissed Armelline's fair hands, and as she felt the contact of my lips her face was suffused by a vivid blush. Never had the lips of man touched more dainty hands before, and she looked quite astounded at the ardour with which I kissed them.

I went home full of love for her, and without heeding the obstacles in my path I gave reins to my passion, which seemed to me the most ardent I had ever experienced.

My young friend was in an ocean of bliss. He had declared his love, and the girl had said that she would gladly become his wife if he could get the cardinal's consent. As this consent only depended on his ability to keep himself, I promised to give him a hundred crowns and my patronage. He had served his time as a tailor's apprentice, and was in a position to open a shop of his own.

"I envy your lot," said I, "for your happiness is assured, while I, though I love your sister, despair of possessing her."

"Are you married then?" he asked.

"Alas, yes! Keep my counsel, for I propose visiting her every day, and if it were known that I was married, my visits would be received with suspicion."

I was obliged to tell this lie to avoid the temptation of marrying her, and to prevent Armelline thinking that I was courting her with that intention.

I found the superioress a polite and clever woman, wholly free from prejudices. After coming down to the grate to oblige me, she sometimes came for her own pleasure. She knew that I was the author of the happy reform in the institution, and she told me that she considered herself under great obligations to me. In less than six weeks three of her girls made excellent marriages, and six hundred crowns had been added to the yearly income of the house.

She told me that she was ill pleased with one of their confessors. He was a Dominican, and made it a rule that his penitents should approach the holy table every Sunday and feast day; he kept them for hours in the confessional, and imposed penances and fastings which were likely to injure the health of young girls.

"All this," said she, "cannot improve them from a mortal point of view, and takes up a lot of their time, so that they have none left for their work, by the sale of which they procure some small comforts for themselves."

"How many confessors have you?"

"Four."

"Are you satisfied with the other three?"

"Yes, they are sensible men, and do not ask too much of poor human nature."

"I will carry your just complaint to the cardinal; will you write out your petition?"

"Kindly give me a model."

I gave her a rough draft, which she copied out and signed, and I laid it before his eminence. A few days after the Dominican was removed, and his penitents divided amongst the three remaining confessors. The younger members of the community owed me a great debt of gratitude on account of this change.

Menicuccio went to see his sweetheart every holiday, while I, in my amorous ardour, visited his sister every morning at nine o'clock. I breakfasted with her and Emilie, and remained in the parlour till eleven. As there was only one grating I could lock the door behind me, but we could be seen from the interior of the convent, as the door was left open to admit light, there being no window. This was a great annoyance for me; recluses, young or old, were continually passing by, and none of them failed to give a glance in the direction of the grate; thus my fair Armelline could not stretch out her hand to receive my amorous kisses.

Towards the end of December the cold became intense, and I begged the superior to allow me to place a screen in front of the door, as I feared I should catch cold otherwise. The worthy woman granted my request without any difficulty, and we were at our ease for the future, though the desires with which Armelline inspired me had become dreadful torment.

On the 1st day of January, 1771, I presented each of them with a good winter dress, and sent the superior a quantity of chocolate, sugar, and coffee, all of which were extremely welcome.

Emilie often came by herself to the grating, as Armelline was not ready, and in the same way Armelline would come by herself when her governess happened to be busy. It was in these quarters of an hour that she succeeded in captivating me, heart and soul.

Emilie and Armelline were great friends, but their prejudices on the subject of sensual enjoyment were so strong that I could never get them to listen to licentious talk, to allow certain small liberties which I would gladly have taken, or to afford me those pleasures of the eyes that we accept in default of better things.

One day they were petrified by my asking them whether they did not sometimes sleep in the same bed, so as to give each other proofs of the tenderness of their mutual affection.

How they blushed Emilie asked me with the most perfect innocence what there was in common between affection and the inconvenience of sleeping two in a narrow bed.

I took care not to explain myself, for I saw that I had frightened them. No doubt they were of the same flesh and blood as I, but our educators had differed widely. They had evidently never confided their little secrets to one another, possibly not even to their confessor, either through shame, or with the idea that the liberties they indulged in alone were no sin.

I made them a present of some silk stockings, lined with plush to keep out the cold, and vainly endeavoured to make them try the stockings on before me. I might say as often as I pleased that there was no real difference between a man's legs and a woman's, and that their confessor would laugh at them if they confessed to shewing their legs. They only answered that girls were not allowed to take such a liberty, as they wore petticoats on purpose to conceal their legs.

The manner in which Emilie spoke, always with Armelline's approbation, convinced me that their modesty was genuine. I penetrated her idea; she thought that in acceding to my request she would be lowering herself in my eyes, and that I should despise her ever after. Nevertheless Emilie was a woman of twenty-seven, and by no means a devotee.

As for Armelline, I could see that she took Emilie for her model, and would have been ashamed of appearing less precise than her friend. I thought she loved me, and that, contrary to the general rule, she would be more easily won by herself than in company with her friend.

I made the trial one morning when she appeared at the grating by herself, telling me that her governess was busy. I said that I adored her and was the most hapless of men, for being a married man I had no hope of ever being able to clasp her to my arms and cover her with kisses.

"Can I continue to live, dear Armelline, with no other consolation than that of kissing your fair hands?"

At these words, pronounced with so much passion, she fixed her gaze on me, and after a few moments' reflection she began to kiss my hands as ardently as I had kissed hers.

I begged her to put her mouth so that I might kiss it. She blushed and looked down, and did nothing. I bewailed my fate bitterly, but in vain. She was deaf and dumb till Emilie came and asked us why we were so dull.

About this time, the beginning of 1771, I was visited by Mariuccia, whom I had married ten years before to a young hairdresser. My readers may remember how I met her at Abbe Momolo's. During the three months I had been in Rome I had enquired in vain as to what had become of her; so that I was delighted when she made her appearance.

"I saw you at St. Peter's," said she, "at the midnight mass on Christmas Eve, but not daring to approach you because of the people with whom I was, I told a friend of mine to follow you and find out where you lived."

"How is it that I have tried to find you out in vain for the last three months?"

"My husband set up at Frascati eight years ago, and we have lived there very happily ever since."

"I am very glad to hear it. Have you any children?"

"Four; and the eldest, who is nine years old, is very like you."

"Do you love her?"

"I adore her, but I love the other three as well."

As I wanted to go to breakfast with Armelline I begged Margarita to   keep Mariuccia company till my return.

Mariuccia dined with me, and we spent a pleasant day together without attempting to renew our more tender relationship. We had plenty to talk about, and she told me that Costa, my old servant, had come back to Rome in a splendid coach, three years after I had left, and that he had married one of Momolo's daughters.

"He's a rascal; he robbed me."

"I guessed as much; his theft did him no good. He left his wife two years after their marriage, and no one knows what has become of him."

"How about his wife?"

"She is living miserably in Rome. Her father is dead."

I did not care to go and see the poor woman, for I could not do anything for her, and I could not have helped saying that if I caught her husband I would do my best to have him hanged. Such was indeed my intention up to the year 1785, when I found this runagate at Vienna. He was then Count Erdich's man, and when we come to that period the reader shall hear what I did.

I promised Mariuccia to come and see her in the course of Lent.

The Princess Santa Croce and the worthy Cardinal Bernis pitied me for my hapless love; I often confided my sufferings to their sympathizing ears.

The cardinal told the princess that she could very well obtain permission from Cardinal Orsini to take Armelline to the theatre, and that if I cared to join the party I might find her less cruel.

"The cardinal will make no objection," said he, "as Armelline has taken no vows; but as you must know our friend's mistress before making your request, you have only to tell the cardinal that you would like to see the interior of the house."

"Do you think he will give me leave?"

"Certainly; the inmates are not cloistered nuns. We will go with you."

"You will come too? that will be a delightful party indeed."

"Ask for leave, and we will arrange the day."

This plan seemed to me a delicious dream. I guessed that the gallant cardinal was curious to see Armelline, but I was not afraid as I knew he was a constant lover. Besides I felt sure that if he took an interest in the fair recluse he would be certain to find her a husband.

In three or four days the princess summoned me to her box in the Alberti Theatre, and shewed me Cardinal Orsini's note, allowing her and her friends to see the interior of the house.

"To-morrow afternoon," said she, "we will fix the day and the hour for the visit."

Next day I paid my usual visit to the recluses, and the superioress came to tell me that the cardinal had told her that the Princess Santa Croce was coming to visit the house with some friends.

"I know it," said I; "I am coming with her."

"When is she coming?"

"I don't know yet, but I will inform you later on."

"This novelty has turned the house upside down. The devotees scarcely know whether they are awake or dreaming, for with the exception of a few priests, the doctor, and the surgeon, no one has ever entered the house since its foundation."

"All these restrictions are now removed, and you need not ask the cardinal's permission to receive visits from your friends."

"I know that, but I don't like to go so far."

The time for the visit was fixed for the afternoon of the next day, and I let the superioress know early the next morning. The Duchess of Fiano had asked to join us; the cardinal came, of course, dressed as a simple priest, with no indication of his exalted rank. He knew Armelline directly from my description, and congratulated her on having made my acquaintance.

The poor girl blushed to the roots of her hair; and I thought she would have fainted when the princess, after telling her she was the prettiest girl in the house, gave her two affectionate kisses, a mark of friendship strictly forbidden by the rules.

After these caresses, the princess proceeded to compliment the superioress. She said that I had done well to praise her parts, as she could judge of them by the order and neatness which reigned everywhere.

"I shall mention your name to Cardinal Orsini," she added, "and you may be sure I shall do you all the justice you deserve."

When we had seen all the rooms, which contained nothing worth seeing, I presented Emilie to the princess, who received her with great cordiality.

"I have heard of your sadness," she said, "but I know the reason of it. You are a good girl, and pretty too, and I shall get you a husband who will cure you of your melancholy."

The superioress gave a smile of approbation, but I saw a dozen aged devotees pulling wry faces.

Emilie dared not reply, but she took the princess's hand and kissed it, as if to summon her to keep her promise.

As for me, I was delighted to see that though all the girls were really pretty, my Armelline eclipsed them all, as the light of the sun obscures the stars.

When we came down to the parlour, the princess told Armelline that she meant to ask leave of the cardinal to take her two or three times to the theatre before Lent began. This observation seemed to petrify everyone except the superioress, who said that his eminence had now a perfect right to relax any or all of the rules of the establishment.

Poor Armelline was so overwhelmed between joy and confusion that she could not speak. She seemed unable to find words wherein to thank the princess, who commended her and her friend Emilie to the superioress before she left the house, and gave her a small present to buy necessaries for them.

Not to be outdone, the Duchess of Fiano told the superioress that she would make me the almoner of her bounty towards Armelline and Emilie. My expressions of gratitude to the princess when we were back in the carriage may be imagined.

I had no need to excuse Armelline, for the princess and the cardinal had gauged her capacities. Her confusion had prevented her shewing her cleverness, but her face shewed her to possess it. Besides, the influence of the education she had received had to be taken into account. The princess was impatient to take her to the theatre, and afterwards to supper at an inn, according to the Roman custom.

She wrote the names of Armelline and Emilie upon her tablets, so as to remember them on every occasion.

I did not forget the mistress of my poor friend Menicuccio, but the time was not opportune for mentioning her name. The next day, however, I got the cardinal's ear, and told him that I was anxious to do something for the young man. The cardinal saw him, and Menicuccio pleased him so well that the marriage took place before the end of the carnival, the bride having a dowry of five hundred crowns. With this sum and the hundred crowns I gave him, he was in a position to open a shop for himself.

The day after the princess's visit was a triumphant one for me. As soon as I appeared at the grating the superioress was sent for, and we had an interview.

The princess had given her fifty crowns, which she was going to lay out on linen for Armelline and Emilie.

The recluses were stupefied when I told them that the fat priest was Cardinal Bernis, as they had an idea that a cardinal can never doff the purple.

The Duchess of Fiano had sent a cask of wine, which was an unknown beverage there, and these presents made them hope for others. I was looked upon as the bringer of all this good luck, and gratitude shewed itself so plainly in every word and glance that I felt I might hope for everything.

A few days later, the princess told Cardinal Orsini that she had taken a peculiar interest in two of the young recluses, and desiring to provide them with suitable establishments she wished to take them now and again to the theatre so as to give them some knowledge of the world. She undertook to take them and bring them back herself or only to confide them to sure hands. The cardinal replied that the superioress should receive instructions to oblige her in every particular.

As soon as I heard of this from the princess, I said that I would ascertain what orders had been actually received at the convent.

The next day the superioress told me that his eminence had instructed her to do what she thought best for the welfare of the young people committed to her charge.

"I have also received orders," she added, "to send in the names of those who have attained the age of thirty, and wish to leave the convent, that they may receive a warrant for their two hundred crowns. I have not yet published this command, but I haven't the slightest doubt that we shall get rid of a score at least."

I told the princess of the cardinal's orders, and she agreed with me that his behaviour was most generous.

Cardinal Bernis, who was by, advised her that the first time she took the girls to the theatre she had better go in person, and tell the superioress that she would always send her carriage and liveried servants to fetch them.

The princess approved of this advice, and a few days later she called for Emilie and Armelline, and brought them to her palace, where I awaited them with the cardinal, the prince, and the Duchess of Fiano.

They were welcomed warmly, encouraged to reply, to laugh, and to say what was in their minds, but all in vain; finding themselves for the first time in a splendid apartment surrounded by brilliant company, they were so confounded that they could not say a word. Emilie persisted in rising from her seat whenever she was addressed, and Armelline shone only by her beauty and the vivid blush which suffused her face whenever she was addressed. The princess might kiss her as much as she pleased, but the novice had not the courage to return her kisses.

At last Armelline mustered up courage to take the princess's hand and kiss it, but when the lady kissed her on the lips the girl remained inactive, seeming to be absolutely ignorant of such a natural and easy matter as the returning of a kiss.

The cardinal and the prince laughed; the duchess said that so much restraint was unnatural. As for me I was on thorns, such awkwardness seemed to me near akin to stupidity, for Armelline had only to do to the princess's lips what she had already done to her hand. No doubt she fancied that to do to the princess what the princess had done to her would shew too much familiarity.

The cardinal took me on one side and said he could not believe that I had not initiated her in the course of two months' intimacy, but I pointed out to him the immense force of long engrained prejudice.

Far this first tine the princess had made up her mind to take them to the Torre di Nonna Theatre, as comic pieces were played there, and they could not help but laugh.

After the play we went to sup at an inn, and at table the good cheer and my exhortations began to take some effect on her. We persuaded them to drink a little wine, and their spirits improved visibly. Emilie ceased to be sad, and Armelline gave the princess some real kisses. We applauded their efforts to be gay and our applause convinced them that they had done nothing wrong.

Of course the princess charged me with the pleasant trust of taking the two guests back to the convent. Now, I thought, my time has come; but when we were in the carriage I saw that I had reckoned without my host. When I would have kissed, heads were turned aside; when I would have stretched forth an indiscreet hand, dresses were wrapped more tightly; when I would have forced my way, I was resisted by force; when I complained, I was told that I was in the wrong; when I got in a rage, I was allowed to say on; and when I threatened to see them no more, they did not believe me.

When we got to the convent a servant opened the side door, and noticing that she did not shut it after the girls, I went in too, and went with them to see the superioress, who was in bed, and did not seem at all astonished to see me. I told her that I considered it my duty to bring back her young charges in person. She thanked me, asked them if they had had a pleasant evening, and bade me good night, begging me to make as little noise as possible on my way downstairs.

I wished them all happy slumbers, and after giving a sequin to the servant who opened the door, and another to the coachman, I had myself set down at the door of my lodging. Margarita was asleep on a sofa and welcomed me with abuse, but she soon found out by the ardour of my caresses that I had not been guilty of infidelity.

I did not get up till noon, and at three o'clock I called on the princess and found the cardinal already there.

They expected to hear the story of my triumph, but the tale I told and my apparent indifference in the matter came as a surprise.

I may as well confess that my face was by no means the index of my mind. However, I did my best to give the thing a comic turn, saying that I did not care for Pamelas, and that I had made up my mind to give up the adventure.

"My dear fellow," said the cardinal, "I shall take two or three days before I congratulate you on your self-restraint."

His knowledge of the human heart was very extensive.

Armelline thought I must have slept till late as she did not see me in the morning as usual; but when the second day went by without my coming she sent her brother to ask if I were ill, for I had never let two days pass without paying her a visit.

Menicuccio came accordingly, and was delighted to find me in perfect health.

"Go and tell your sister," I said, "that I shall continue to interest the princess on her behalf, but that I shall see her no more."

"Why not?"

"Because I wish to cure myself of an unhappy passion. Your sister does not love me: I am sure of it. I am no longer a young man, and I don't feel inclined to become a martyr to her virtue. Virtue goes rather too far when it prevents a girl giving the man who adores her a single kiss."

"Indeed, I would not have believed that of her."

"Nevertheless it is the fact, and I must make an end of it. Your sister cannot understand the danger she runs in treating a lover in this fashion. Tell her all that, my dear Menicuccio, but don't give her any advice of your own."

"You can't think how grieved I am to hear all this; perhaps it's Emilie's presence that makes her so cold."

"No; I have often pressed her when we have been alone together, but all in vain. I want to cure myself, for if she does not love me I do not wish to obtain her either by seduction or by any feeling of gratitude on her part. Tell me how your future bride treats you."

"Very well, ever since she has been sure of my marrying her."

I felt sorry then that I had given myself out as a married man, for in my state of irritation I could even have given her a promise of marriage without deliberately intending to deceive her.

Menicuccio went on his way distressed, and I went to the meeting of the "Arcadians," at the Capitol, to hear the Marchioness d'Aout recite her reception piece. This marchioness was a young Frenchwoman who had been at Rome for the last six months with her husband, a man of many talents, but inferior to her, for she was a genius. From this day I became her intimate friend, but without the slightest idea of an intrigue, leaving all that to a French priest who was hopelessly in love with her, and had thrown up his chances of preferment for her sake.

Every day the Princess Santa Croce told me that I could have the key to her box at the theatre whenever I liked to take Armelline and Emilie, but when a week passed by without my giving any sign she began to believe that I had really broken off the connection.

The cardinal, on the other hand, believed me to be still in love, and praised my conduct. He told me that I should have a letter from the superioress, and he was right; for at the end of the week she wrote me a polite note begging me to call on her, which I was obliged to obey.

I called on her, and she began by asking me plainly why my visits had ceased.

"Because I am in love with Armelline."

"If that reason brought you here every day, I do not see how it can have suddenly operated in another direction."

"And yet it is all quite natural; for when one loves one desires, and when one desires in vain one suffers, and continual suffering is great unhappiness. And so you see that I am bound to act thus for my own sake."

"I pity you, and see the wisdom of your course; but allow me to tell you that, esteeming Armelline, you have no right to lay her open to a judgment being passed upon her which is very far from the truth."

"And what judgment is that?"

"That your love was only a whim, and that as soon as it was satisfied you abandoned her."

"I am sorry indeed to hear of this, but what can I do? I must cure myself of this unhappy passion. Do you know any other remedy than absence? Kindly advise me."

"I don't know much about the affection called love, but it seems to me that by slow degrees love becomes friendship, and peace is restored."

"True, but if it is to become friendship, love must be gently treated. If the beloved object is not very tender, love grows desperate and turns to indifference or contempt. I neither wish to grow desperate nor to despise Armelline, who is a miracle of beauty and goodness. I shall do my utmost for her, just as if she had made me happy, but I will see her no more."

"I am in complete darkness on the matter. They assure me that they have never failed in their duty towards you, and that they cannot imagine why you have ceased coming here."

"Whether by prudence, or timidity, or a delicate wish not to say anything against me, they have told you a lie; but you deserve to know all, and my honour requires that I should tell you the whole story."

"Please do so; you may count on my discretion."

I then told my tale, and I saw she was moved.

"I have always tried," she said, "never to believe evil except on compulsion, nevertheless, knowing as I do the weakness of the human heart, I could never have believed that throughout so long and intimate an acquaintance you could have kept yourself so severely within bounds. In my opinion there would be much less harm in a kiss than in all this scandal."

"I am sure that Armelline does not care about it."

"She does nothing but weep."

"Her tears probably spring from vanity, or from the cause her companions assign for my absence."

"No, I have told them all that you are ill."

"What does Emilie say?"

"She does not weep, but she looks sad, and says over and over again that it is not her fault if you do not come, thereby hinting that it is Armelline's fault. Come tomorrow to oblige me. They are dying to see the opera at the Aliberti, and the comic opera at the Capronica."

"Very good, then I will breakfast with them to-morrow morning, and to-morrow evening they shall see the opera."

"You are very good; I thank you. Shall I tell them the news?"

"Please tell Armelline that I am only coming after hearing all that you have said to me."

The princess skipped for joy when she heard of my interview with the superioress, and the cardinal said he had guessed as much. The princess gave me the key of her box, and ordered that her carriage and servants should be at my orders.

The next day when I went to the convent Emilie came down by herself to reproach me on my cruel conduct. She told me that a man who really loved would not have acted in such a manner, and that I had been wrong to tell the superioress everything.

"I would not have said anything if I had had anything important to say."

"Armelline has become unhappy through knowing you."

"Because she does not want to fail in her duty, and she sees that you only love her to turn her from it."

"But her unhappiness will cease when I cease troubling her."

"Do you mean you are not going to see her any more?"

"Exactly. Do you think that it costs me no pain? But I must make the effort for the sake of my peace of mind."

"Then she will be sure that you do not love her."

"She must think what she pleases. In the meanwhile I feel sure that if she loved me as I loved her, we should be of one mind."

"We have duties which seem to press lightly on you."

"Then be faithful to your duties, and permit a man of honour to respect them by visiting you no more."

Armelline then appeared. I thought her changed.

"Why do you look so grave and pale?"

"Because you have grieved me."

"Come then, be gay once more, and allow me to cure myself of a passion, the essence of which is to induce you to fail in your duty.

I shall be still your friend, and I shall come to see you once a week while I remain in Rome."

"Once a week! You needn't have begun by coming once a day."

"You are right; it was your kind expression which deceived me, but I hope you will allow me to become rational again. For this to happen, I must try not to see you more than I can help. Think over it, and you will see that I am doing all for the best."

"It's very hard that you can't love me as I love you."

"You mean calmly, and without desires."

"I don't say that; but holding your desires in check, if they are contrary to the voice of duty."

"I'm too old to learn this method, and it does not seem to me an attractive one. Kindly tell me whether the restraint of your desires gives you much pain?"

"I don't repress my desires when I think of you, I cherish them; I wish you were the Pope, I wish you were my father, that I might caress you in all innocence; in my dreams I wish you could become a girl, so that we might always live happily together."

At this true touch of native simplicity, I could not help smiling.

I told them that I should come in the evening to take them to the Aliberti, and felt in a better humour after my visit, for i could see that there was no art or coquetry in what Armelline said. I saw that she loved me, but would not come to a parley with her love, hence her repugnance to granting me her favours; if she once did so, her eyes would be opened. All this was pure nature, for experience had not yet taught her that she ought either to avoid me or to succumb to my affection.

In the evening I called for the two friends to take them to the opera, and I had not long to wait. I was by myself in the carriage, but they evinced no surprise. Emilie conveyed to me the compliments of the superioress, who would be obliged by my calling on her the following day. At the opera I let them gaze at the spectacle which they saw for the first time, and answered whatever questions they put to me. As they were Romans, they ought to have known what a castrato was, nevertheless, Armelline took the wretched individual who sang the prima donna's part for a woman, and pointed to his breast, which was really a fine one.

"Would you dare to sleep in the same bed with him?" I asked.

"No; an honest girl ought always to sleep by herself."

Such was the severity of the education they had received. Everything connected with love was made a mystery of, and treated with a kind of superstitious awe. Thus Armelline had only let me kiss her hands after a long contest, and neither she nor Emilie would allow me to see whether the stockings I had given them fitted well or not. The severe prohibition that was laid on sleeping with another girl must have made them think that to shew their nakedness to a companion would be a great sin, and let a man see their beauties a hideous crime. The very idea of such a thing must have given them a shudder.

Whenever I had attempted to indulge in conversation which was a little free, I had found them deaf and dumb.

Although Emilie was a handsome girl in spite of her pallor, I did not take sufficient interest in her to try to dissipate her melancholy; but loving Armelline to desperation I was cut to the quick to see her look grave when I asked her if she had any idea of the difference between the physical conformation of men and women.

As we were leaving Armelline said she was hungry, as she had scarcely eaten anything for the last week on account of the grief I had given her.

"If I had foreseen that," I answered, "I would have ordered a good supper, whereas I have now only potluck to offer you."

"Never mind. How many shall we be?"

"We three."

"So much the better; we shall be more at liberty."

"Then you don't like the princess?"

"I beg your pardon, but she wants me to kiss her in a way I don't like."

"Nevertheless, you kissed her ardently enough."

"I was afraid she would take me for a simpleton if I did not do so."

"Then do you think you committed a sin in kissing her like that?"

"Certainly not, for it was very unpleasant for me."

"Then why won't you make the same effort on my behalf?"

She said nothing, and when we got to the inn I ordered them to light a fire and to get a good supper ready.

The waiter asked me if I would like some oysters, and noticing the curiosity of my guests on the subject I asked him how much they were.

"They are from the arsenal at Venice," he replied, "and we can't sell them under fifty pains a hundred."

"Very good, I will take a hundred, but you must open them here."

Armelline was horrified to think that I was going to pay five crowns for her whim, and begged me to revoke the order; but she said nothing when I told her that no pleasure of hers could be bought too dearly by me.

At this she took my hand and would have carried it to her lips, but I took it away rather roughly, greatly to her mortification.

I was sitting in front of the fire between them, and I was sorry at having grieved her.

"I beg pardon, Armelline," I said, "I only took my hand away because it was not worthy of being carried to your fair lips."

In spite of this excuse she could not help two big tears coursing down her blushing cheeks. I was greatly pained.

Armelline was a tender dove, not made to be roughly treated. If I did not want her to hate me I felt that I must either not see her at all or treat her more gently for the future.

Her tears convinced me that I had wounded her feelings terribly, and I got up and went out to order some champagne.

When I came back I found that she had been weeping bitterly. I did not know what to do; I begged her again and again to forgive me, and to be gay once more, unless she wished to subject me to the severest of all punishments.

Emilie backed me up, and on taking her hand and covering it with kisses, I had the pleasure of seeing her smile once more.

The oysters were opened in our presence, and the astonishment depicted on the girls' countenances would have amused me if my heart had been more at ease. But I was desperate with love, and Armelline begged me vainly to be as I was when we first met.

We sat down, and I taught my guests how to suck up the oysters, which swam in their own liquid, and were very good.

Armelline swallowed half a dozen, and then observed to her friend that so delicate a morsel must be a sin.

"Not on account of its delicacy," said Emilie, "but because at every mouthful we swallow half a Paul."

"Half a Paul!" said Armelline, "and the Holy Father does not forbid such a luxury? If this is not the sin of gluttony, I don't know what is. These oysters are delightful; but I shall speak about the matter to my director."

These simplicities of hers afforded me great mental pleasure, but I wanted bodily pleasure as well.

We ate fifty oysters, and drank two bottles of sparkling champagne, which made my two guests eruct and blush and laugh at the same time.

I would fain have laughed too and devoured Armelline with my kisses,   but I could only devour her with by eyes.

I kept the remainder of the oysters for dessert, and ordered the supper to be served. It was an excellent meal, and the two heroines enjoyed it; even Emilie became quite lively.

I ordered up lemons and a bottle of rum, and after having the fifty remaining oysters opened I sent the waiter away. I then made a bowl of punch, pouring in a bottle of champagne as a finishing touch.

After they had swallowed a few oysters and drank one or two glasses of punch, which they liked amazingly, I begged Emilie to give me an oyster with her lips.

"I am sure you are too sensible to find anything wrong in that," I added.

Emilie was astonished at the proposition, and thought it over. Armelline gazed at her anxiously, as if curious as to how she would answer me.

"Why don't you ask Armelline?" she said at length.

"Do you give him one first," said Armelline, "and if you have the courage
I will try to do the same."

"What courage do you want? It's a child's game; there's no harm in it."

After this reply, I was sure of victory. I placed the shell on the edge of her lips, and after a good deal of laughing she sucked in the oyster, which she held between her lips. I instantly recovered it by placing my lips on hers.

Armelline clapped her hands, telling Emilie that she would never have thought her so brave; she then imitated her example, and was delighted with my delicacy in sucking away the oyster, scarcely touching her lips with mine. My agreeable surprise may be imagined when I heard her say that it was my turn to hold the oysters. It is needless to say that I acquitted myself of the duty with much delight.

After these pleasant interludes we went to drinking punch and swallowing oysters.

We all sat in a row with our backs to the fire, and our brains began to whirl, but never was there such a sweet intoxication. However, the punch was not finished and we were getting very hot.

I took off my coat, and they were obliged to unlace their dresses, the bodices of which were lined with fur. Guessing at necessities which they did not dare to mention, I pointed out a closet where they could make themselves comfortable, and they went in hand-in-hand. When they came out they were no longer timid recluses, they were shrieking with laughter, and reeling from side to side.

I was their screen as we sat in front of the fire, and I gazed freely on charms which they could no longer conceal. I told them that we must not think of going till the punch was finished, and they agreed, saying, in high glee, that it would be a great sin to leave so good a thing behind.

I then presumed so far as to tell them that they had beautiful legs, and that I should be puzzled to assign the prize between them. This made them gayer than ever, for they had not noticed that their unlaced bodices and short petticoats let me see almost everything.

After drinking our punch to the dregs, we remained talking for half an hour, while I congratulated myself on my self-restraint. Just as we were going I asked them if they had any grounds of complaint against me. Armelline replied that if I would adopt her as my daughter she was ready to follow me to the end of the world. "Then you are not afraid of my turning you from the path of duty?"

"No, I feel quite safe with you."

"And what do you say, dear Emilie?"

"I shall love you too, when you do for me what the superioress will tell you to-morrow."

"I will do anything, but I shan't come to speak to her till the evening, for it is three o'clock now."

They laughed all the louder, exclaiming,—

"What will the mother say?"

I paid the bill, gave something to the waiter, and took them back to the convent, where the porteress seemed well enough pleased with the new rules when she saw two sequins in her palm.

It was too late to see the superioress, so I drove home after rewarding the coachman and the lackey.

Margarita was ready to scratch my eyes out if I could not prove my fidelity, but I satisfied her by quenching on her the fires Armelline and the punch had kindled. I told her I had been kept by a gaming party, and she asked no more questions.

The next day I amused the princess and the cardinal by a circumstantial account of what had happened.

"You missed your opportunity," said the princess.

"I don't think so," said the cardinal, "I believe, on the contrary, that he has made his victory more sure for another time."

In the evening, I went to the convent where the superioress gave me her warmest welcome. She complimented me on having amused myself with the two girls till three o'clock in the morning without doing anything wrong. They had told her how we had eaten the oysters, and she said it was an amusing idea. I admired her candour, simplicity, or philosophy, whichever you like to call it.

After these preliminaries, she told me that I could make Emilie happy by obtaining, through the influence of the princess, a dispensation to marry without the publication of banns a merchant of Civita Vecchia, who would have married her long ago only that there was a woman who pretended to have claims upon him. If banns were published this woman would institute a suit which might go on forever.

"If you do this," she concluded, "you will have the merit of making Emilie happy."

I took down the man's name, and promised to do my best with the princess.

"Are you still determined to cure yourself of your love for Armelline?"

"Yes, but I shall not begin the cure till Lent."

"I congratulate you; the carnival is unusually long this year."

The next day I spoke of the matter to the princess. The first requisite was a certificate from the Bishop of Civita Vecchia, stating that the man was free to marry. The cardinal said that the man must come to Rome, and that the affair could be managed if he could bring forward two good witnesses who would swear that he was unmarried.

I told the superioress what the cardinal said, and she wrote to the merchant, and a few days after I saw him talking to the superioress and Emilie through the grating.

He commended himself to my protection, and said that before he married he wanted to be sure of having six hundred crowns.

The convent would give him four hundred crowns, so we should have to obtain a grant of two hundred more.

I succeeded in getting the grant, but I first contrived to have another supper with Armelline, who asked me every morning when I was going to take her to the comic opera. I said I was afraid of turning her astray from the path of duty, but she replied that experience had taught her to dread me no longer.

CHAPTER XVII

The Florentine—Marriage of Emilie—Scholastica—Armelline at the Ball

Before the supper I had loved Armelline to such an extent that I had determined to see her no more, but after it I felt that I must obtain her or die. I saw that she had only consented to my small liberties because she regarded them as mere jokes, of no account, and I resolved to take advantage of this way of looking at it to go as far as I could. I begin to play the part of indifferent to the best of my ability, only visiting her every other day, and looking at her with an expression of polite interest. I often pretended to forget to kiss her hand, while I kissed Emilie's and told her that if I felt certain of receiving positive marks of her affection I should stay at Civita Vecchia for some weeks after she was married. I would not see Armelline's horror, who could not bear me to take a fancy to Emilie.

Emilie said that she would be more at liberty when she was married, while Armelline, vexed at her giving me any hopes, told her sharply that a married woman had stricter duties to perform than a girl.

I agreed with her in my heart, but as it would not have suited my purpose to say so openly I insinuated the false doctrine that a married woman's chief duty is to keep her husband's descent intact, and that everything else is of trifling importance.

With the idea of driving Emilie to an extremity I told Emilie that if she wanted me to exert myself to my utmost for her she must give me good hopes of obtaining her favours not only after but before marriage.

"I will give you no other favours." she replied, "than those which Armelline may give you. You ought to try to get her married also."

In spite of her grief at these proposals, gentle Armelline replied,——

"You are the only man I have ever seen; and as I have no hopes of getting married I will give you no pledges at all, though I do not know what you mean by the word."

Though I saw how pure and angelic she was, I had the cruelty to go away, leaving her to her distress.

It was hard for me to torment her thus, but I thought it was the only way to overcome her prejudices.

Calling on the Venetian ambassador's steward I saw some peculiarly fine oysters, and I got him to let me have a hundred. I then took a box at the Capronica Theatre, and ordered a good supper at the inn where we had supped before.

"I want a room with a bed," I said to the waiter.

"That's not allowed in Rome, signor," he replied, "but on the third floor we have two rooms with large sofas which might do instead, without the Holy Office being able to say anything."

I looked at the rooms and took them, and ordered the man to get the best supper that Rome could offer.

As I was entering the boa with the two girls I saw the Marchioness d'Aout was my near neighbour. She accosted me, and congratulated herself on her vicinity to me. She was accompanied by her French abbe, her husband, and a fine-looking young man, whom I had never seen before. She asked who my companions were, and I told her they were in the Venetian ambassador's household. She praised their beauty and began to talk to Armelline, who answered well enough till the curtain went up. The young man also complimented her, and after having asked my permission he gave her a large packet of bonbons, telling her to share them with her neighbour. I had guessed him to be a Florentine from his accent, and asked him if the sweets came from the banks of the Arno; he told me they were from Naples, whence he had just arrived.

At the end of the first act I was surprised to hear him say that he had a letter of introduction for me from the Marchioness of C——.

"I have just heard your name," he said, "and tomorrow I shall have the honour of delivering the letter in person, if you will kindly give me your address."

After these polite preliminaries I felt that I must comply with his request.

I asked after the marquis, his mother-in-law, and Anastasia, saying that I was delighted to hear from the marchioness from whom I had been expecting an answer for the last month.

"The charming marchioness has deigned to entrust me with the answer you speak of."

"I long to read it."

"Then I may give you the letter now, though I shall still claim the privilege of calling on you to-morrow. I will bring it to you in your box, if you will allow me."

"Pray do so."

He might easily have given it to me from the box where he was, but this would not have suited his plans. He came in, and politeness obliged me to give him my place next to Armelline. He took out an elaborate pocket-book, and gave me the letter. I opened it, but finding that it covered four pages, I said I would read it when I got home, as the box was dark. "I shall stay in Rome till Easter," he said, "as I want to see all the sights; though indeed I cannot hope to see anything more beautiful than the vision now before me."

Armelline, who was gazing fixedly at him, blushed deeply. I felt that his compliment, though polite, was entirely out of place, and in some sort an insult to myself. However, I said nothing, but decided mentally that the Florentine Adonis must be a fop of the first water.

Finding his compliment created a silence, he saw he had made himself offensive, and after a few disconnected remarks withdrew from the box. In spite of myself the man annoyed me, and I congratulated Armelline on the rapidity of her conquest, asking her what she thought of him. "He is a fine man, but his compliments shews he has no taste. Tell me, is it the custom for people of fashion to make a young girl blush the first time they see her?"

"No, dear Armelline, it is neither customary nor polite; and anyone who wishes to mix in good society would never do such a thing."

I lapsed into silence, as though I wanted to listen to the music; but as a matter of fact my heart was a prey to cruel jealousy. I thought the matter over, and came to the conclusion that the Florentine had treated me rudely. He might have guessed that I was in love with Armelline, and to make such an open declaration of love to my very face was nothing more nor less than an insult to me.

After I had kept this unusual silence for a quarter of an hour the simple Armelline made me worse by saying that I must calm myself, as I might be sure that the young man's compliment had not given her the slightest pleasure. She did not see that by saying this she made me feel that the compliment had had the directly opposite effect.

I said that I had hoped he had pleased her.

To finish the matter up, she said by way of soothing me that the young man did not mean to vex me, as he doubtless took me for her father.

What could I reply to this observation, as cruel as it was reasonable? Nothing; I could only take refuge in silence and a fit of childish ill-humour.

At last I could bear it no longer, and begged the two girls to come away with me.

The second act was just over, and if I had been in my right senses I should never have made them such an unreasonable request; but the crassness of my proceedings did not strike me till the following day.

In spite of the strangeness of my request they merely exchanged glances and got ready to go. Not knowing what better excuse to give I told them I did not want the princess's carriage to be noticed as everyone left the theatre, and that I would bring them again to the theatre the following day.

I would not let Armelline put her head inside the Marchioness d'Aout's box, and so we went out. I found the man who accompanied the carriage talking to one of his mates at the door of the theatre, and this made me think that the princess had come to the opera.

We got down at the inn, and I whispered to the man to take his horses home and to call for us at three o'clock; for the cold was intense, and both horses and men had to be considered.

We began by sitting down in front of a roaring fire, and for half an hour we did nothing but eat oysters, which were opened in our presence by a clever waiter, who took care not to lose a drop of the fluid. As quick as he opened we ate, and the laughter of the girls, who talked of how we had eaten them before, caused my anger to gradually disappear.

In Armelline's gentleness I saw the goodness of her heart, and I was angry with myself for my absurd jealousy of a man who was much more calculated to please a young girl than I.

Armelline drank champagne, and stole occasional glances in my direction as if to entreat me to join them in their mirth.

Emilie spoke of her marriage, and without saying anything about my projected visit to Civita Vecchia I promised that her future husband should have his plenary dispensation before very long. While I spoke I kissed Armelline's fair hands, and she looked at me as if thankful for the return of my affection.

The oysters and champagne had their natural effect, and we had a delightful supper. We had sturgeon and some delicious truffles, which I enjoyed not so much for my own sake as for the pleasure with which my companions devoured them.

A man in love is provided with a kind of instinct which tells him that the surest way to success is to provide the beloved object with pleasures that are new to her.

When Armelline saw me become gay and ardent once more she recognized her handiwork, and was doubtless proud of the power she exercised over me. She took my hand of her own accord, and continued gazing into my eyes. Emilie was occupied in the enjoyment of the meal, and did not trouble herself about our behaviour. Armelline was so tender and loving that I made sure of victory after we had had some more oysters and a bowl of punch.

When the dessert, the fifty oysters, and all the materials for making the punch were on the table, the waiter left the room, saying that the ladies would find every requisite in the neighbouring apartment.

The room was small, and the fire very hot, and I bade the two friends arrange their dress more comfortably.

Their dresses fitted their figures, and were trimmed with fur and stiffened with whalebones, so they went into the next room, and came back in white bodices and short dimity petticoats, laughing at the slightness of their attire.

I had sufficient strength of mind to conceal my emotion, and even not to look at their breasts when they complained of having no neckerchiefs or breast-bands to their chemises. I knew how inexperienced they were, and felt certain that when they saw the indifference with which I took their slight attire they themselves would think it was of no consequence. Armelline and Emilie had both beautiful breasts, and knew it; they were therefore astonished at my indifference, perhaps thought that I had never seen a fine breast. As a matter of fact a fine figure is much more scarce at Rome than a pretty face.

Thus, in spite of their modesty, their vanity impelled them to shew me that my indifference was ill-placed, but it was my part to put them at their ease, and to make them fling shame to the winds.

They were enchanted when I told them to try their hands at a bowl of punch, and they simply danced for joy when I pronounced it better than my own brew.

Then came the oyster-game, and I scolded Armelline for having swallowed the liquid as I was taking the oyster from her lips. I agreed that it was very hard to avoid doing so, but I offered to shew them how it could be done by placing the tongue in the way. This gave me an opportunity of teaching them the game of tongues, which I shall not explain because it is well known to all true lovers. Armelline played her part with such evident relish that I could see she enjoyed it as well as I, though she agreed it was a very innocent amusement.

It so chanced that a fine oyster slipped from its shell as I was placing it between Emilie's lips. It fell on to her breast, and she would have recovered it with her fingers; but I claimed the right of regaining it myself, and she had to unlace her bodice to let me do so. I got hold of the oyster with my lips, but did so in such a manner as to prevent her suspecting that I had taken any extraordinary pleasure in the act. Armelline looked on without laughing; she was evidently surprised at the little interest I had taken in what was before my eye. Emilie laughed and relaced her bodice.

The opportunity was too good to be lost, so taking Armelline on my knee I gave her an oyster and let it slip as Emilie's had slipped, much to the delight of the elder, who wanted to see how her young companion would go through the ordeal.

Armelline was really as much delighted herself, though she tried to conceal her pleasure.

"I want my oyster," said I.

"Take it, then."

There was no need to tell me twice. I unlaced her corset in such a way as to make it fall still lower, bewailing the necessity of having to search for it with my hands.

What a martyrdom for an amorous man to have to conceal his bliss at such a moment!

I did not let Armelline have any occasion to accuse me of taking too much licence, for I only touched her alabaster spheres so much as was absolutely necessary.

When I had got the oyster again I could restrain myself no more, and affixing my lips to one of the blossoms of her breast I sucked it with a voluptuous pleasure which is beyond all description.

She was astonished, but evidently moved, and I did not leave her till my enjoyment was complete.

When she marked my dreamy langourous gaze, she asked me it it had given me much pleasure to play the part of an infant.

"Yes, dearest," I replied, "but it's only an innocent jest."

"I don't think so; and I hope you will say nothing about it to the superioress. It may be innocent for you, but it is not for me, as I experienced sensations which must partake of the nature of sin. We will pick up no more oysters."

"These are mere trifles," said Emilie, "the stain of which will easily be wiped out with a little holy water. At all events we can swear that there has been no kissing between us."

They went into the next room for a moment, I did the same, and we then sat on the sofa before the fire. As I sat between them I observed that our legs were perfectly alike, and that I could not imagine why women stuck so obstinately to their petticoats.

While I talked I touched their legs, saying it was just as if I were to touch my own.

They did not interrupt this examination which I carried up to the knee, and I told Emilie that all the reward I would ask for my services was that I might see her thighs, to compare them with Armelline's.

"She will be bigger than I," said Armelline, "though I am the taller."

"Well, there would be no harm in letting me see."

"I think there would."

"Well, I will feel with my hands."

"No, you would look at the same time."

"I swear I will not."

"Let me bandage your eyes."

"Certainly; but I will: bandage yours too."

"Yes; we will play, at blindman's buff."

Before the bandaging began I took care to make them swallow a good dose of punch, and, then we proceeded to play. The two girls

---

let me span their thighs several times, laughing and falling over me whenever my hands went too high.

I lifted the bandage and saw everything, but they pretended not to suspect anything.

They treated me in the same way, no doubt to see what it was that they felt when they fell upon me.

This delightful game went on; till exhausted, nature would not allow me to play it any more. I put myself in a state of decency, and then told them to take off their bandages.

They did so and sat beside me, thinking, perhaps, that they would be able to, disavow everything on the score of the bandage.

It seemed to me that Emilie had had a lover, though I took good care not to tell her so; but Armelline was a pure virgin. She was meeker than her friend, and her great eyes shone as voluptuously but more modestly.

I would have snatched a kiss from her pretty mouth, but she turned away her head, though she squeezed my hands tenderly. I was astonished at this refusal after the liberties I had taken with her.

We had talked about balls, and they were both extremely anxious to see one.

The public ball was the rage with all the young Romans. For ten long years the Pope Rezzonico had deprived them of this pleasure. Although Rezzonico forbade dancing, he allowed gaming of every description. Ganganelli, his successor, had other views, and forbade gaming but allowed dancing.

So much for papal infallibility; what one condemns the other approves. Ganganelli thought it better to let his subjects skip than to give them the opportunity of ruining themselves, of committing suicide, or of becoming brigands; but Rezzonico did not see the matter in that light. I promised the girls I would take them to the ball as soon as I could discover one where I was not likely to be recognized.

Three o'clock struck, and I took them back to the convent, well enough pleased with the progress I had made, though I had only increased my passion. I was surer than ever that Armelline was born to exercise an irresistible sway over every man who owed fealty to beauty.

I was amongst her liegemen, and am so still, but the incense is all gone and the censer of no value.

I could not help reflecting on the sort of glamour which made me fall in love with one who seemed all new to me, while I loved her in exactly the same manner as I had loved her predecessor. But in reality there was no real novelty; the piece was the same, though the title might be altered. But when I had won what I coveted, did I realize that I was going over old ground? Did I complain? Did I think myself deceived?

Not one whit; and doubtless for this reason, that whilst I enjoyed the piece I kept my eyes fixed on the title which had so taken my fancy. If this be so, of what use is title at all? The title of a book, the name of a dish, the name of a town—of what consequence are all these when what one wants is to read the book, to eat the dish, and to see the town.

The comparison is a sophism. Man becomes amorous through the senses, which, touch excepted, all reside in the head. In love a beautiful face is a matter of the greatest moment.

A beautiful female body might well excite a man to carnal indulgence, even though the head were covered, but never to real love. If at the moment of physical delight the covering were taken away, and a face of hideous, revolting ugliness disclosed, one would fly in horror, in spite of the beauties of the woman's body.

But the contrary does not hold good. If a man has fallen in love with a sweet, enchanting face, and succeeds in lifting the veil of the sanctuary only to find deformities there, still the face wins the day, atones for all, and the sacrifice is consummated.

The face is thus paramount, and hence it has come to be agreed that women's bodies shall be covered and their faces disclosed; while men's clothes are arranged in such a way that women can easily guess at what they cannot see.

This arrangement is undoubtedly to the advantage of women; art can conceal the imperfections of the face, and even make it appear beautiful, but no cosmetic can dissemble an ugly breast, stomach, or any other part of the man body.

In spite of this, I confess that the phenomerides of Sparta were in the right, like all women who, though they possess a fine figure, have a repulsive face; in spite of the beauty of the piece, the title drives spectators away. Still an interesting face is an inseparable accident of love.

Thrice happy are they who, like Armelline, have beauty both in the face and body.

When I got home I was so fortunate as to find Margarita in a deep sleep. I took care not to awake her, and went to bed with as little noise as possible. I was in want of rest, for I no longer enjoyed the vigour of youth, and I slept till twelve.

When I awoke, Margarita told me that a handsome young man had called on me at ten o'clock, and that she had amused him till eleven, not daring to awake me.

"I made him some coffee," said she, "and he was pleased to pronounce it excellent. He would not tell me his name, but he will come again tomorrow. He gave me a piece of money, but I hope you will not mind. I don't know how much it is worth."

I guessed that it was the Florentine. The piece was of two ounces. I only laughed, for not loving Margarita I was not jealous of her. I told her she had done quite right to amuse him and to accept the piece, which was worth forty-eight pauls.

She kissed me affectionately, and thanks to this incident I heard nothing about my having come home so late.

I felt curious to learn more about this generous Tuscan, so I proceeded to read Leonilda's letter.

His name, it appeared, was M——. He was a rich merchant established   in London, and had been commended to her husband by a Knight of Malta.

Leonilda said he was generous, good-hearted, and polished, and assured me that I should like him.

After telling me the family news, Leonilda concluded by saying that she was in a fair way to become a mother, and that she would be perfectly happy if she gave birth to a son. She begged me to congratulate the marquis.

Whether from a natural instinct or the effects of prejudice, this news made me shudder. I answered her letter in a few days, enclosing it in a letter to the marquis, in which I told him that the grace of God was never too late, and that I had never been so much pleased by any news as at hearing he was likely to have an heir.

In the following May Leonilda gave birth to a son, whom I saw at Prague, on the occasion of the coronation of Leopold. He called himself Marquis C——, like his father, or perhaps we had better say like his mother's husband, who attained the age of eighty.

Though the young marquis did not know my name, I got introduced to him, and had the pleasure of meeting him a second time at the theatre. He was accompanied by a priest, who was called his governor, but such an office was a superfluity for him, who was wiser at twenty than most men are at sixty.

I was delighted to see that the young man was the living image of the old marquis. I shed tears of joy as I thought how this likeness must have pleased the old man and his wife, and I admired this chance which seemed to have abetted nature in her deceit.

I wrote to my dear Leonilda, placing the letter in the hands of her son. She did not get it till the Carnival of 1792, when the young marquis returned to Naples; and a short time after I received an answer inviting me to her son's marriage and begging me to spend the remainder of my days with her.

"Who knows? I may eventually do so."

I called on the Princess Santa Croce at three o'clock, and found her in bed, with the cardinal reading to her.

The first question she asked was, why I had left the opera at the end of the second act.

"Princess, I can tell you an interesting history of my six hours of adventure, but you must give me a free hand, for some of the episodes must be told strictly after nature."

"Is it anything in the style of Sister M—— M——?" asked the cardinal.

"Yes, my lord, something of the kind."

"Princess, will you be deaf?" said his eminence,

"Of course I will," she replied.

I then told my tale almost as I have written it. The slipping oysters and the game of blind man's buff made the princess burst with laughing, in spite of her deafness. She agreed with the cardinal that I had acted with great discretion, and told me that I should be sure to succeed on the next attempt.

"In three or four days," said the cardinal, "you will have the dispensation, and then Emilie can marry whom she likes."

The next morning the Florentine came to see me at nine o'clock, and I found him to answer to the marchioness's description; but I had a bone to pick with him, and I was none the better pleased when he began asking me about the young person in my box at the theatre; he wanted to know whether she were married or engaged, if she had father, mother, or any other relations.

I smiled sardonically, and begged to be excused giving him the required information, as the young lady was masked when he saw her.

He blushed, and begged my pardon.

I thanked him for doing Margarita the honour of accepting a cup of coffee from her hands, and begged him to take one with me, saying I would breakfast with him next morning. He lived with Roland, opposite St. Charles, where Madame Gabrieli, the famous singer, nicknamed la Coghetta, lived.

As soon as the Florentine was gone, I went to St. Paul's in hot haste, for I longed to see what reception I should have from the two vestals I had initiated so well.

When they appeared I noticed a great change. Emilie had become gay, while Armelline looked sad.

I told the former that she should have her dispensation in three days, and her warrant for four hundred crowns in a week.

"At the same time," I added, "you shall have your grant of two hundred crowns."

At this happy tidings she ran to tell the superioress of her good fortune.

As soon as I was alone with Armelline I took her hands and covered them with kisses, begging her to resume her wonted gaiety.

"What shall I do," said she, "without Emilie? What shall I do when you are gone? I am unhappy. I love myself no longer."

She shed tears which pierced me to the heart. I swore I would not leave
Rome till I had seen her married with a dowry of a thousand crowns.

"I don't want a thousand crowns, but I hope you will see me married as you say; if you do not keep your promise it will kill me."

"I would die rather than deceive you; but you on your side must forgive my love, which, perhaps, made me go too far the other evening."

"I forgive you everything if you will remain my friend."

"I will; and now let me kiss your beautiful lips."

After this first kiss, which I took as a pledge of certain victory, she wiped away her tears; and soon after Emilie reappeared, accompanied by the superioress, who treated me with great cordiality.

"I want you to do as much for Armelline's new friend as you have done for Emilie," said she.

"I will do everything in my power," I replied; "and in return I hope you will allow me to take these young ladies to the theatre this evening."

"You will find them ready; how could I refuse you anything?"

When I was alone with the two friends I apologised for having disposed of them without their consent.

"Our consent!" said Emilie: "we should be ungrateful indeed if we refused you anything after all you have done for us."

"And you, Armelline, will you withstand my love?"

"No; so long as it keeps within due bounds. No more blind man's buff!"

"And it is such a nice game! You really grieve me."

"Well, invent another game," said Emilie.

Emilie was becoming ardent, somewhat to my annoyance, for I was afraid Armelline would get jealous. I must not be charged with foppishness on this account. I knew the human heart.

When I left them I went to the Tordinona Theatre and took a box, and then ordered a good supper at the same inn, not forgetting the oysters, though I felt sure I should not require their aid.

I then called on a musician, whom I requested to get me three tickets for a ball, where no one would be likely to know me.

I went home with the idea of dining by myself, but I found a note from the Marchioness d'Aout, reproaching me in a friendly manner for not having broken bread with her, and inviting me to dinner. I resolved to accept the invitation, and when I got to the house I found the young Florentine already there.

It was at this dinner that I found out many of his good qualities, and I saw that Donna Leonilda had not said too much in his favour.

Towards the end of the meal the marchioness asked why I had not stayed till the end of the opera.

"Because the young ladies were getting tired."

"I have found out that they do not belong to the Venetian ambassador's household."

"You are right, and I hope you will pardon my small fiction."

"It was an impromptu effort to avoid telling me who they are, but they are known."

"Then I congratulate the curious."

"The one I addressed deserves to excite general curiosity; but if I were in your place I should make her use a little powder."

"I have not the authority to do so, and if I had, I would not trouble her for the world."

I was pleased with the Florentine, who listened to all this without saying a word. I got him to talk of England and of his business. He told me that he was going to Florence to take possession of his inheritance, and to get a wife to take back with him to London. As I left, I told him that I could not have the pleasure of calling on him till the day after next, as I was prevented by important business. He told me I must come at dinnertime, and I promised to do so.

Full of love and hope, I went for my two friends, who enjoyed the whole play without any interruption.

When we alighted at the inn I told the coachman to call for me at two, and we then went up to the third floor, where we sat before the fire while the oysters were being opened. They did not interest us as they had done before.

Emilie had an important air; she was about to make a good marriage. Armelline was meek, smiling, and affectionate, and reminded me of the promise I had given her. I replied by ardent kisses which reassured her, while they warned her that I would fain increase the responsibility I had already contracted towards her. However, she seemed resigned, and I sat down to table in a happy frame of mind.

As Emilie was on the eve of her wedding, she no doubt put down my neglect of her to my respect for the sacrament of matrimony.

When supper was over I got on the sofa with Armelline, and spent three hours which might have been delicious if I had not obstinately endeavoured to obtain the utmost favour. She would not give in; all my supplications and entreaties could not move her; she was sweet, but firm. She lay between my arms, but would not grant what I wanted, though she gave me no harsh or positive refusal.

It seems a puzzle, but in reality it is quite simple.

She left my arms a virgin, sorry, perhaps, that her sense of duty had not allowed her to make me completely happy.

At last nature bade me cease, in spite of my love, and I begged her to forgive me. My instinct told me that this was the only way by which I might obtain her consent another time.

Half merry and half sad, we awoke Emilie who was in a deep sleep, and then we started. I went home and got into bed, not troubling myself about the storm of abuse with which Margarita greeted me.

The Florentine gave me a delicious dinner, overwhelmed me with protestations of friendship, and offered me his purse if I needed it.

He had seen Armelline, and had been pleased with her. I had answered him sharply when he questioned me about her, and ever since he had never mentioned her name.

I felt grateful to him, and as if I must make him some return.

I asked him to dinner, and had Margarita to dine with us. Not caring for her I should have been glad if he had fallen in love with her; there would have been no difficulty, I believe, on her part, and certainly not on mine; but nothing came of it. She admired a trinket which hung from his watch-chain, and he begged my permission to give it her. I told him to do so by all means, and that should have been enough; but the affair went no farther.

In a week all the arrangements for Emilie's marriage had been made. I gave her her grant, and the same day she was married and went away with her husband to Civita Vecchia. Menicuccio, whose name I have not mentioned for some time, was well pleased with my relations with his sister, foreseeing advantages for himself, and still better pleased with the turn his own affairs were taking, for three days after Emilie's wedding he married his mistress, and set up in a satisfactory manner. When Emilie was gone the superioress gave Armelline a new companion. She was only a few years older than my sweetheart, and very pretty; but she did not arouse a strong interest in my breast. When violently in love no other woman has ever had much power over me.

The superioress told me that her name was Scholastica, and that she was well worthy of my esteem, being, as she said, as good as Emilie. She expressed a hope that I would do my best to help

Scholastica to marry a man whom she knew and who was in a good position.

This man was the son of a cousin of Scholastica's. She called him her nephew, though he was older than she. The dispensation could easily be got for money, but if it was to be had for nothing I should have to make interest with the Holy Father. I promised I would do my best in the matter.

The carnival was drawing to a close, and Scholastica had never seen an opera or a play. Armelline wanted to see a ball, and I had at last succeeded in finding one where it seemed unlikely that I should be recognized. However, it would have to be carefully managed, as serious consequences might ensue; so I asked the two friends if they would wear men's clothes, to which they agreed very heartily.

I had taken a box at the Aliberti Theatre for the day after the ball, so I told the two girls to obtain the necessary permission from the superioress.

Though Armelline's resistance and the presence of her new friend discouraged me, I procured everything requisite to transform them into two handsome lads.

As Armelline got into the carriage she gave me the bad news that Scholastica knew nothing about our relations, and that we must be careful what we did before her. I had no time to reply, for Scholastica got in, and we drove off to the inn. When we were seated in front of a good fire, I told them that if they liked I would go into the next room in spite of the cold.

So saying, I shewed them their disguises, and Armelline said it would do if I turned my back, appealing to Scholastics to confirm her.

"I will do as you like," said she, "but I am very sorry to be in the way. You are in love with each other, and here am I preventing you from giving one another marks of your affection. Why don't you treat me with confidence? I am not a child, and I am your friend."

These remarks shewed that she had plenty of common sense, and I breathed again.

"You are right, fair Scholastics," I said, "I do love Armelline, but she does not love me, and refuses to make me happy on one pretence or another."

With these words I left the room, and after shutting the door behind me proceeded to make up a fire in the second apartment.

In a quarter of an hour Armelline knocked at the door, and begged me to open it. She was in her breeches, and said they needed my assistance as their shoes were so small they could not get them on.

I was in rather a sulky humour, so she threw her arms round my neck and covered my face with kisses which soon restored me to myself.

While I was explaining the reason of my ill temper, and kissing whatever
I could see, Scholastica burst out laughing.

"I was sure that I was in the way," said she; "and if you do not trust me, I warn you that I will not go with you to the opera to-morrow."

"Well, then, embrace him," said Armelline.

"With all my heart."

I did not much care for Armelline's generosity, but I embraced Scholastica as warmly as she deserved. Indeed I would have done so if she had been less pretty, for such kindly consideration deserved a reward. I even kissed her more ardently than I need have done, with the idea of punishing Armelline, but I made a mistake. She was delighted, and kissed her friend affectionately as if in gratitude.

I made them sit down, and tried to pull on their shoes, but I soon found that they were much too small, and that we must get some more.

I called the waiter who attended to us, and told him to go and fetch a bootmaker with an assortment of shoes.

In the meanwhile I would not be contented with merely kissing Armelline. She neither dared to grant nor to refuse; and as if to relieve herself of any responsibility, made Scholastica submit to all the caresses I lavished on her. The latter seconded my efforts with an ardour that would have pleased me exceedingly if I had been in love with her.

She was exceedingly beautiful, and her features were as perfectly chiselled as Armelline's, but Armelline was possessed of a delicate and subtle charm of feature peculiar to herself.

I liked the amusement well enough, but there was a drop of bitterness in all my enjoyment. I thought it was plain that Armelline did not love me, and that Scholastica only encouraged me to encourage her friend.

At last I came to the conclusion that I should do well to attach myself to the one who seemed likely to give me the completest satisfaction.

As soon as I conceived this idea I felt curious to see whether Armelline would discover any jealousy if I shewed myself really in love with Scholastica, and if the latter pronounced me to be too daring, for hitherto my hands had not crossed the Rubicon of their waistbands. I was just going to work when the shoemaker arrived, and in a few minutes the girls were well fitted.

They put on their coats, and I saw two handsome young men before me, while their figures hinted their sex sufficiently to make a third person jealous of my good fortune.

I gave orders for supper to be ready at midnight, and we went to the ball. I would have wagered a hundred to one that no one would recognize me there, as the man who got the tickets had assured me that it was a gathering of small tradesmen. But who can trust to fate or chance?

We went into the hall, and the first person I saw was the Marchioness d'Aout, with her husband and her inseparable abbe.

No doubt I turned a thousand colours, but it was no good going back, for the marchioness had recognized me, so I composed myself and went up to her. We exchanged the usual compliments of polite society, to which she added some good-natured though ironical remarks on my two young friends. Not being accustomed to company, they remained confused and speechless. But the worst of all was to come. A tall young lady who had just finished a minuet came up to Armelline, dropped a curtsy, and asked her to dance.

In this young lady I recognized the Florentine who had disguised himself as a girl, and looked a very beautiful one.

Armelline thought she would not appear a dupe, and said she recognized him.

"You are making a mistake," said he, calmly. "I have a brother who is very like me, just as you have a sister who is your living portrait. My brother had the pleasure of exchanging a few words with her at the Capronica." The Florentine's cleverness made the marchioness laugh, and I had to join in her mirth, though I felt little inclination to do so.

Armelline begged to be excused dancing, so the marchioness made her sit between the handsome Florentine and herself. The marquis took possession of Scholastica, and I had to be attentive to the marchioness without seeming to be aware of the existence of Armelline, to whom the Florentine was talking earnestly.

I felt as jealous as a tiger; and having to conceal my rage under an air of perfect satisfaction, the reader may imagine how well I enjoyed the ball.

However, there was more anxiety in store for me; for presently I noticed Scholastica leave the marquis, and go apart with a middle-aged man, with whom she conversed in an intimate manner.

The minuets over, the square dances began, and I thought I was dreaming when I saw Armelline and the Florentine taking their places.

I came up to congratulate them, and asked Armelline, gently, if she was sure of the steps.

"This gentleman says I have only to imitate him, and that I cannot possibly make any mistakes."

I had nothing to say to this, so I went towards Scholastica, feeling very curious to know who was her companion.

As soon as she saw me she introduced me to him, saying timidly that this was the nephew of whom she had spoken, the same that wished to marry her.

I was surprised, but I did not let it appear. I told him that the superioress had spoken of him to me, and that I was thinking over the ways and means of obtaining a dispensation without any costs.

He was an honest-looking man, and thanked me heartily, commending himself to my good offices, as he said he was far from rich.

I left them together, and on turning to view the dance I was astonished to see that Armelline was dancing admirably, and executing all the figures. The Florentine seemed a finished dancer, and they both looked very happy.

I was far from pleased, but I congratulated them both on their performance. The Florentine had disguised himself so admirably that no one would have taken him for a man. It was the Marchioness d'Aout who had been his dresser.

As I was too jealous to leave Armelline to her own devices, I refused to dance, preferring to watch her.

I was not at all uneasy about Scholastica, who was with her betrothed. About half-past eleven the Marchioness d'Aout, who was delighted with Armelline, and possibly had her protege's happiness in view, asked me, in a tone that amounted to a command, to sup with her in company with my two companions.

"I cannot have the honour," I replied, "and my two companions know the reason."

"That is as much as to say," said the marchioness, "that he will do as you please," turning to Armelline as she spoke.

I addressed myself to Armelline, and observed smilingly that she knew perfectly well that she must be home by half-past twelve at latest.

"True," she replied, "but you can do as you please."

I replied somewhat sadly that I did not feel myself at liberty to break my word, but that she could make me do even that if she chose.

Thereupon the marchioness, her husband, the abbe, and the Florentine, urged her to use her power to make me break my supposed word, and Armelline actually began to presume to do so.

I was bursting with rage; but making up my mind to do anything rather than appear jealous, I said simply that I would gladly consent if her friend would consent also.

"Very well," said she, with a pleased air that cut me to the quick, "go and ask her."

That was enough for me. I went to Scholastica and told her the circumstances in the presence of her lover, begging her to refuse without compromising me.

Her lover said I was perfectly right, but Scholastica required no persuasion, telling me that she had quite made up her mind not to sup with anyone.

She came with me, and I told her to speak to Armelline apart before saying anything to the others.

I led Scholastica before the marchioness, bewailing my want of success.

Scholastica told Armelline that she wanted to say a few words to her aside, and after a short conversation they came back looking sorry, and Armelline told the marchioness that she found it would be impossible for them to come. The lady did not press us any longer, so we went away.

I told Scholastica's intended to keep what had passed to himself, and asked him to dine with me on the day after Ash Wednesday.

The night was dark, and we walked to the place where I had ordered the carriage to be in waiting.

To me it was as if I had come out of hell, and on the way to the inn I did not speak a word, not even answering the questions which the too-simple Armelline addressed to me in a voice that would have softened a heart of stone. Scholastica avenged me by reproaching her for having obliged me to appear either rude or jealous, or a breaker of my word.

When we got to the inn Armelline changed my jealous rage into pity; her eyes swam with tears, which Scholastica's home truths had drawn forth.

The supper was ready, so they had no time to change their dress. I was sad enough, but I could not bear to see Armelline sad also. I resolved to do my best to drive away her melancholy, even though I suspected that it arose from love of the Florentine.

The supper was excellent, and Scholastica did honour to it, while Armelline, contrary to her wont, scarcely touched a thing. Scholastica was charming. She embraced her friend, and told her to be merry with her, as I had become the friend of her betrothed, and she was sure I would do as much for her as I had done for Emilie. She blessed the ball and the chance which had brought him there. In short, she did her best to shew Armelline that with my love she had no reason to be sad.

Armelline dared not disclose the true cause of her sadness. The fact was, that she wanted to get married, and the handsome Florentine was the man to her liking.

Our supper came to an end, and still Armelline was gloomy. She only drank one glass of punch, and as she had eaten so little I would not try and make her drink more for fear lest it should do her harm. Scholastica, on the other hand, took such a fancy to this agreeable fluid, which she tasted for the first time, that she drank deeply, and was amazed to find it mounting to her head instead of descending to her stomach. In this pleasant state, she felt it was her duty to reconcile Armelline and myself, and to assure us that we might be as tender as we liked without minding her presence.

Getting up from table and standing with some difficulty, she carried her friend to the sofa, and caressed her in such a way that Armelline could not help laughing, despite her sadness. Then she called me and placed her in my arms. I caressed her, and Armelline, though she did not repulse me, did not respond as Scholastica had hoped. I was not disappointed; I did not think it likely she would grant now what she had refused to grant when I had held her in my arms for those hours whilst Emilie was fast asleep.

However, Scholastica began to reproach me with my coldness, though I deserved no blame at all on this score.

I told them to take off their men's clothes, and to dress themselves as women.

I helped Scholastica to take off her coat and waistcoat, and then aided
Armelline in a similar manner.

When I brought them their chemises, Armelline told me to go and stand by the fire, and I did so.

Before long a noise of kissing made me turn round, and I saw Scholastica, on whom the punch had taken effect, devouring Armelline's breast with kisses. At last this treatment had the desired result; Armelline became gay, and gave as good as she got.

At this sight the blood boiled in my veins, and running to them I found Scholastic was not ill pleased that I should do justice to her beautiful spheres, while for the nonce I transformed her into a nurse.

Armelline was ashamed to appear less generous than her friend, and Scholastica was triumphant when she saw the peculiar use to which (for the first time) I put Armelline's hands.

Armelline called to her friend to help, and she was not backward; but in spite of her twenty years her astonishment at the catastrophe was great.

After it was over I put on their chemises and took off their breeches with all the decency imaginable, and after spending a few minutes in the next room they came and sat down on my knee of their own accord.

Scholastica, instead of being annoyed at my giving the preference to the hidden charms of Armelline, seemed delighted, watching what I did, and how Armelline took it, with the closest attention. She no doubt longed to see me perform the magnum opus, but the gentle Armelline would not allow me to go so far.

After I had finished with Armelline I recollected I had duties towards
Scholastica, and I proceeded to inspect her charms.

It was difficult to decide which of the two deserved to carry off the apple. Scholastica, perhaps, was strictly speaking the more beautiful of the two, but I loved Armelline, and love casts a glamour over the beloved object. Scholastica appeared to me to be as pure a virgin as Armelline, and I saw that I might do what I liked with her. But I would not abuse my liberty, not caring to confess how powerful an ally the punch had been.

However, I did all in my power to give her pleasure without giving her the greatest pleasure of all. Scholastica, was glutted with voluptuous enjoyment, and was certain that I had only eluded her desires from motives of delicacy.

I took them back to the convent, assuring them that I would take them to the opera on the following evening.

I went to bed, doubtful whether I had gained a victory or sustained a defeat; and it was not till I awoke that I was in a position to give a decided opinion.

[There is here a considerable hiatus in the author's manuscript.]

The End

www.ingramcontent.com/pod-product-compliance
Lightning Source LLC
Chambersburg PA
CBHW070009300526
45794CB00001B/251